Chicago's Famous Buildings

Chicago's

Fourth Edition, Revised and Enlarged

Famous Buildings

A Photographic Guide to the

City's Architectural Landmarks

and Other Notable Buildings

Edited by Franz Schulze

and Kevin Harrington

The University of Chicago Press Chicago & London

Franz Schulze is professor emeritus of art at Lake Forest College and author of *Mies van der Rohe: A Critical Biography,* published by the University of Chicago Press.
Kevin Harrington is professor of humanities and architecture at the Illinois Institute of Technology.

Publication of this book was made possible by a generous grant from the Graham Foundation for Advanced Studies in the Fine Arts.

The University of Chicago Press, Chicago 60637
The University of Chicago Press, Ltd., London
© 1965, 1969, 1980, 1993 by The University of Chicago
All rights reserved.
Published 1965; second edition 1969; third edition 1980; fourth edition 1993
Printed in the United States of America
02 01 00 99 98 97 96 95   2 3 4 5 6

ISBN (cloth): 0–226–74061–7
ISBN (paper): 0–226–74062–5

Library of Congress Cataloging-in-Publication Data

Chicago's famous buildings : a photographic guide to the city's
   architectural landmarks and other notable buildings.—4th ed. /
   edited by Franz Schulze and Kevin Harrington.
      p.   cm.
   Includes index.
      1. Architecture—Illinois—Chicago—Guidebooks.   2. Public
   buildings—Illinois—Chicago—Guidebooks.   3. Chicago (Ill.)—
   Buildings, structures, etc.—Guidebooks.   I. Schulze, Franz,
   1927– . II. Harrington, Kevin, 1944– .
   NA735.C4C4   1993
   720'.09773'11—dc20   92–26334
                                                          CIP

This book is printed on acid-free paper.

Contents

While this book is inspired by the illustrious record of architecture in Chicago, it is old enough to have a history in its own right—moreover one that extends back more than a generation. First published in 1965, it appears now in its fourth edition, and a review of its contents over the years offers an insight into the shifts of values and tastes that have motivated the architects who built the city and the scholars and critics who have studied their accomplishments.

In large part the first edition grew out of the organization in the 1950s of the Commission on Chicago Landmarks. As such, its attention was focused on cherished individual buildings (hence the title of the book), particularly those associated with the Chicago school, a body of technically inventive, formally bold, and straightforward work from the late nineteenth and early twentieth centuries that was credited with shaping much of the modern architectural aesthetic and elevating designers like Louis Sullivan, Daniel Burnham, John Wellborn Root, Frank Lloyd Wright, and Ludwig Mies van der Rohe to an exalted position in the textbooks. These men were celebrated not only as exemplary masters but as revolutionaries, whose efforts, Ira Bach wrote in the foreword to the first edition, added up to "the most important innovation in the art of building since the Gothic cathedrals."

Bach's superlative was in step with mainstream critical thought of the mid-1960s. The success of the first edition and the acceptance of its point of view were apparent in the publication just four years later, in 1969, of the second edition, which differed from its predecessor only in the extensiveness of its coverage. It made room for a number of newly erected buildings that seemed to constitute a revival of the old Chicago school and for the suburban work of Frank Lloyd Wright and his followers.

In the third edition, of 1980, on the other hand, a significantly altered outlook was discernible. The Chicago school was no longer taken as the prime measure of quality in Chicago building, nor was the historic importance of the city's architecture rated so high or asserted so apodictically. Historicist as well as modernist buildings were included and organization followed geographical lines rather than stylistic or technical categories. Not only individual buildings but whole areas or neighborhoods, often of collective or anonymous as distinct from singular authorship, were cited. If not explicit, the more broadly accommodating attitude called post-modernism, so influential in international thinking about architecture in the last decade, can now be retrospectively inferred from passages in the third edition.

In turn, this fourth edition is comparably reflective of the period that gave birth to it, even if we as the editors would like to believe we are free of the bondage of the moment. Yet the very recognition that critical objectivity is a difficult, not to say impossible condition to sustain is typical of history writing in the 1990s. We have endeavored to be fair in our revision of *Chicago's Famous Buildings*, but we are aware that in walking the tightrope between comprehensiveness and discrimination we have exercised our respective personal judgments. And the fifth edition, which is certain to succeed the fourth, will likewise and ineluctably yield to the biases of its time.

All that notwithstanding, we share the fundamental conviction of earlier editions that Chicago is a collective architectural treasure and exceptional in many respects, not least the undiminished brilliance of the aforementioned individual designers and some of their contemporaries and followers. At the same time, conscious of the city's *genius loci,* we argue that Chicago owes its architectural reputation to much of its planning as well as many of its buildings, to the vernacular of its outlying neighborhoods and the widely varied makeup of its suburban landscape as well as to the glittering towers of its commercial core. Meanwhile, we are also obliged to acknowledge—as earlier, more optimistic Chicago generations were loath to do—that any study of the city's built environment must take into account failures as obviously shortsighted as the repeated demolition of some of its greatest buildings and as grimly profound as the latter-day collapse of much of its inner city.

In our efforts we have also continued to hold in high esteem those devoted, keenly informed students of Chicago history who made this book possible in the first place, especially the previous editors, Arthur Siegel and Ira Bach, and the contributors to its text (much of which we have retained), J. Carson Webster, Carl W. Condit, Wilbert R. Hasbrouck, Hugh Dalziel Duncan, and Roy Forrey. We wish to express our gratitude for the sustained support of the Graham Foundation for Advanced Studies in the Fine Arts. Special thanks are also due to Carter H. Manny, Jr., and Tim Samuelson for their scrupulous reading of the text.

Lastly, in recollection of the history of this book, we have studiously kept its format and title. It is a handbook, meant to be concise rather than encyclopedic, and intended for a place in a pedestrian's tote bag or a motorist's glove compartment, not alone on a library shelf. And it is first and finally about *buildings:* the essential object and objective of the art and craft of architecture.

Chicago's buildings have enjoyed international fame for more than a century, though the character of the matrix for these distinguished works has been continually transformed during that time. Members of the American Institute of Architects surveyed recently judged Chicago the city with the finest architecture in the nation. When this guidebook was initiated almost thirty years ago, the central concern was to provide access to the significant buildings of the first and second Chicago schools of architecture. These schools have been defined as developing a frankly modern architecture, free of subservience to the past, combined with work that expressed the metal frame as a source of order in large commercial buildings and the wooden balloon frame as a source of freedom in suburban houses. Since the 1970s the buildings that make Chicago famous have come to include many neither designed nor influenced by either the Chicago or the Prairie school.

For us, Chicago's buildings continue to excite interest for reasons that relate to a variety of qualities we associate with the city. They are not unique to Chicago, but the particular combination they exhibit here contributes powerfully to its sense of place. The extraordinarily open space and light of the site have also found expression in its buildings. While the skyscrapers' regular and open frames with their broad sheets of glass display an interest in the simultaneously transparent and reflective qualities of the glass in conveying images of space and light, buildings constructed along traditional masonry lines also suppress the expression of the mass of the building, emphasizing instead the thinness of the wall planes and the abundance of glazed surfaces that describe the psychological relation between open and enclosed space. Chicago buildings are also notable for the high level of detail, or craft, or finish accorded them. This derives from the demands of the architects, the pride of the construction workers, and the expectations of the developers. The standards set early on have attracted architects eager to meet those standards, whether they have chosen to live here or simply been invited to contribute some work. That many of the most distinguished names in architecture have built in Chicago testifies to this. These include H. H. Richardson, Louis Sullivan, Dankmar Adler, Frank Lloyd Wright, John Root, Daniel Burnham, and Ludwig Mies van der Rohe, as well as such lesser known, but often equally gifted architects as Howard Van Doren Shaw, William Holabird, Martin Roche, David Adler, Bertrand Goldberg, Myron Goldsmith, Fazlur Khan, Walter Netsch, Bruce Graham, Harry Weese, Jacques Brownson, Gene Summers, Helmut Jahn, Ralph Johnson, and Thomas Beeby. In addition the leading architecture firms that have emerged in Chicago have also developed means to control the quality of their work, so that Burnham & Root, an office striving for the main chance, could produce masterpieces such as the Monadnock, or the symbol of corporate architecture in the late twentieth century, Skidmore, Owings & Merrill, could produce a work of the power of the John Hancock or the grace of the Inland Steel. Finally, architects in Chicago have been interested in architecture, whether in the city or elsewhere, and so they have sought to undertake the most demanding challenges as they have pursued their work.

However, as great as many of the individual buildings are, the background buildings of Chicago are of exceptionally high quality. Architecture is the city's greatest art form, and this has set a standard that all those who practice here recognize and seek to emulate. This effort is best repaid when architects are confident of their gifts rather than seeking to address and surpass other models.

For a city distinguished in part by the considerable height of its buildings, the 6 feet that divide the continent between the Mississippi and Great Lakes watersheds on the southwest side of Chicago hardly seem to matter. But it is just that ease of crossing the natural boundaries of the continent that attracted first Native Americans and later ambitious immigrants from the rest of the world to the city whose name has been said to mean "swamp," "smelly place," or "wild onion." This site, promising the easy exchange of commodities, culture, and ideas, has been continually reinforced in the two centuries of Chicago's growth—first with waterborne shipping, later with railroads, then with the motor car and truck, and most recently with air traffic. Even power distribution networks—the electrical distribution grid, the natural gas pipeline system—and information systems—telegraph, telephone (copper wire, fiber optic or cellular and microwave communications)—have also reinforced this vast manmade crossroads of Chicago.

Bearing a Native American name, first settled by Jean Pointe Baptiste Du Sable, a man of African and European heritage who came to trade, the city has primarily been a place of manufacture, commerce, and trade. The great public interest institutions of the city—libraries, universities, museums, and symphonies—have grown because Chicago provided opportunities for enormous material success. The presence of the federal and state governments has been relatively minor, expanding dramatically only in the last quarter of a century. The city and county governments have seen it as their responsibility to ease the achievement of the desires of those who wished to build in Chicago. When corruption has from time to time sustained enough attention, separate agencies have been created—park commission, forest preserves, public building commissions. Such entities reinforce the view that the public agencies necessary to organize and coordinate development in the region are expected to facilitate the achievement of essentially privately generated vision. There is no expectation that a dominating vision could emerge from the public sector.

At least since the time of George Pullman, the city has witnessed the competition between people of wealth and power who wish to do well for their employees and organizations of those employees who prefer to look after themselves, without the help of paternalistic owners. After nearly a century of trying to ignore the city's black population, shortly after World War II the white power structure began to address some of their needs, often through the means of new housing. The results were decidedly mixed. The developments on Chicago's near South Side of the Prairie Shores and Lake Meadows apartment groups and the somewhat later Stateway Gardens and Robert Taylor housing complexes illustrate how a similar architectural idea—tall apartment buildings widely separated in an open landscape—could have radically different social consequences.

The flatness of the site, the pliancy of the river, and the vastness of the lake seemed to receive the mile-square grid of the Northwest Ordinance as an extremely loose fabric into and through which a metropolis could be woven. Since the ordinance was developed to define an agricultural republic, it offered the same neutral form for towns and cities. Lands for public purposes—schools and local government—were determined by a combination of abstract formulas and ideas of urban hierarchy. Small towns, especially county seats, developed a combined political and commercial focus on and around the courthouse square. But for a great city, which was not imagined by the creators of this pattern, the grid was still void of hierarchy, focus, or large-scale urban order.

In the absence of either a natural or formal hierarchy, Chicago grew in an amorphous manner, leading visitors to see it as chaotic if predictable. From Burnham's plan to the present, designers have been trying to impose order and focus with varying degrees of success. Chicago's stunning natural resource, the lake, with its continuous shoreline of beautiful parks, exists because the lake has been constantly filled in to achieve it. The development of coherent areas emerged from the relation, built up over time, of the buildings with one another and the spaces they collectively define and create, rather than derived from either the character of the site or the focus of the urban plan.

Often, along LaSalle Street or Printer's Row for instance, these spaces are narrow and help define the street. Occasionally, for example at the Federal Center or in Daley Plaza, these spaces emerge as the result of redevelopment. In still other circumstances, along the river or in Grant Park, these spaces have developed into happy amenities after first being treated in an offhand and cavalier manner.

It is a truism that a building must be experienced for itself, in real time, in person. Photographs may give us an idea of a building's appearance, but only a personal visit will permit full understanding. If this is true of individual buildings, it is even more the case for the environments identified here. Even the most sophisticated observer of graphic images would find it difficult to identify the great spaces and places of the city reliably. Once in the city, however, one would find it difficult not to appreciate the quality of these places. Images of other cities—the mountain range of Manhattan, the interconnected squares of London, the radial boulevards of Paris, the broadly encompassing ring of Vienna, the fortuitous tightness of Strasbourg, the interconnected imperial and papal order of Rome—are unable to explain Chicago. This is a new urban form, derived less from any generalized concept and more from the individual quality of its famous buildings.

MAP **1** CHICAGO AND SUBURBS

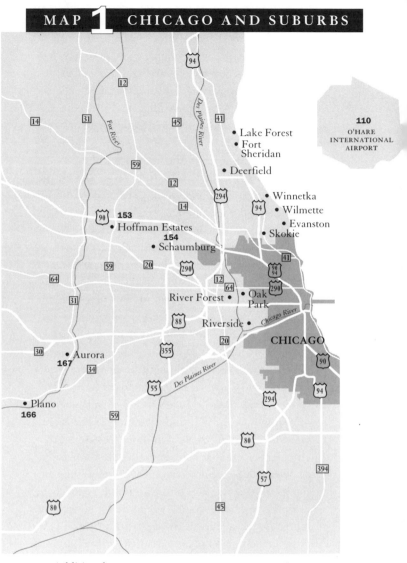

Additional maps on pages 12, 174, 175, 255, 256

MAP **2** CITY OF CHICAGO

The Commercial Core

The intersection of people, goods, and services that encouraged the expansion of Chicago was enormously increased by an astonishing population explosion in the middle of the nineteenth century. From a census of 3,000 in the 1830s, the decade of its incorporation, to 300,000 in the 1870s, the decade when it burned, to 1,000,000 in 1890 and more than 3,000,000 in 1930, the absolute and relative rates of Chicago's growth were staggering. This influx created immense pressure on the central business area for vast quantities of new construction.

The buildings that resulted from the demand, and which over time have served to reinforce it, emerged from a complex web of forces, including personal ambitions of both clients and architects, technological change, an absence of powerful existing forms or constraints on new ideas, reinforced by the psychological as much as physical impact of the Great Fire of 1871. Chicago and other American cities that experienced similar growth following the Civil War were inventing themselves and had few models to emulate. The nearly square blocks of the Loop, served by alleys, were transformed from many small buildings lining the streets to vastly larger buildings covering most if not all of their blocks. The walls of these buildings came to dominate the public space of the city as they defined linear rooms open to the sky. In the absence of a hierarchical sequence, the new spaces of the city developed their individuality only over time and largely through the shared nature of the commerce centered in particular areas. Thus, State Street acquired its character through the concentration of great department stores, while Michigan Avenue developed its imposing cliff overlooking the Lake, and the LaSalle Street canyon burgeoned around the city's commodity and financial markets.

An aspect of the city's transformation through immigration is that architects themselves were not likely to be Chicago natives, whether the great figures of the turn of the century—Burnham, Sullivan, Wright, Root, Atwood, all born elsewhere—or figures of the more recent past—from Mies van der Rohe to Helmut Jahn, likewise born elsewhere and attracted to the city by the opportunities it presented. As immigrants they tended to repeat the experience of Sullivan, who declared as soon as he arrived, "This is the place for me." Chicago had the ability to seem unfinished and capable of being reimagined again and again. The slab skyscrapers of the 1890s were succeeded by the square donut high rises of the 1900s and 1910s to be followed by the stepped-back towers of the 1920s. After the hiatus between the Depression and World War II, the clear frames of Mies exerted their power for several decades, to be succeeded most recently by a generation of stone-veneered and tassel-topped towers. Designers were inclined to imagine that they could redesign the city in the process of rebuilding it. Burnham's challenge to make no little plans has done more to fire the imagination of others than to encourage them to implement his ideas.

Chicago benefits from this richness of buildings. Whether the most prominent or the most reticent, whether the stripped class of office buildings or the more generously ornamented class of public buildings, the ambition of owners to realize the full value of their investments has established a tradition of high quality in materials, details, and realization in the city's large buildings.

The business center of Chicago is undergoing a major expansion and transformation. The discussion of such distinct places as the LaSalle Street canyon shows how a developed area can strengthen its identity over time. Michigan Avenue north of the river is becoming the third major retail center of the city, succeeding State Street, which had in turn supplanted Lake Street. This shift has meant the decline of State Street as a well-defined place in the urban fabric. Whether a place inheres in the city's form or not is often the result of its distinguished architecture, but in the case of Dearborn Street "place" has not occurred. From the river to its train station Dearborn has the single greatest concentration of extraordinary buildings in the city, and yet it has not become a place, in spite of the three distinguished plazas erected along the street in the last generation. The Loop itself has continued to expand to the west, as well as the east along the main branch of the river, while the vast railroad yards below the Loop, which had created a southern wall of high rises as strong if not so well known as the Michigan Avenue wall, have now been transformed for over a decade by the introduction of low- and medium-rise residential development. Finally, Bertrand Goldberg's projects began a pattern of introducing dwellings downtown, a district formerly notable for its very small number of residents. Loft development is strongest around Printer's Row and in the warehouse zone to the west of the Loop. In addition, Michigan Avenue has seen the growth of both residential and office high rises, often in mixed-use developments.

Although the central business district has expanded in the last generation, it has still retained its focus and concentration, thanks to both natural features—river and lake—and man-made elements—rail and road. Since the telegraph, it has been argued that the concentration of central cities would become unnecessary. Nevertheless, the demand for rapid and varied face-to-face contact among people of greatly varying interests and needs remains, and Chicago's Loop continues to provide ease of contact as its core has expanded without beginning to sprawl.

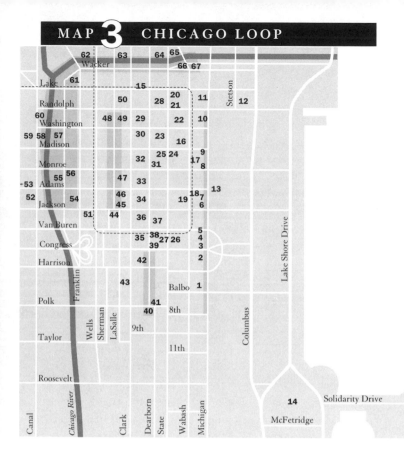

MAP 3 CHICAGO LOOP

Wacker
Lake
Randolph
Washington
Madison
Monroe
Adams
Jackson
Van Buren
Congress
Harrison
Polk
Taylor
Roosevelt

Canal
Chicago River
Franklin
Wells
Sherman
LaSalle
Clark
Dearborn
State
Wabash
Michigan
Columbus
Lake Shore Drive
Stetson

9th
8th
Balbo
11th
McFetridge
Solidarity Drive

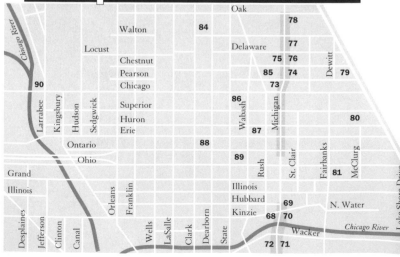

MAP 4 MICHIGAN AVENUE

Oak
Walton
Locust
Chestnut
Pearson
Chicago
Superior
Huron
Erie
Ontario
Ohio
Grand
Illinois
Hubbard
Kinzie
Delaware
Dewitt
N. Water
Wacker

Chicago River
Larrabee
Kingsbury
Hudson
Sedgwick
Orleans
Franklin
Wells
LaSalle
Clark
Dearborn
State
Wabash
Michigan
Rush
St. Clair
Fairbanks
McClurg
Desplaines
Jefferson
Clinton
Canal
Lake Shore Drive
Chicago River

Michigan Avenue Cliff

Chicago Hilton and Towers (1927)
Originally the Stevens Hotel, later the Conrad Hilton
720 South Michigan Avenue
Architects: Holabird & Roche

1 Blackstone Hotel

Columbia College (1907)
Originally Fairbanks-Morse Building
600 South Michigan Avenue
Architect: Christian A. Eckstorm

2 Congress Hotel

3 Auditorium Building

4 Fine Arts Building

5 Chicago Club Building

McCormick Building (1911)
332 South Michigan Avenue
Architects: Holabird & Roche

Britannica Center (1924)
Originally Straus Building
310 South Michigan Avenue
Architects: Graham, Anderson, Probst & White

6 Railway Exchange Building

7 Orchestra Hall

Borg-Warner Building (1958)
200 South Michigan Avenue
Architects: William Lescaze with A. Epstein & Sons

Peoples Gas Building (1911)
122 South Michigan Avenue
Architects: D. H. Burnham & Co.

Lake View Building (1906)
116 South Michigan Avenue
Architects: Jenney, Mundie & Jensen

Illinois Athletic Club (1908)
112 South Michigan Avenue
Architects: Barnett, Haynes & Barnett

Monroe Building (1912)
104 South Michigan Avenue
Architects: Holabird & Roche

8 University Club

9 Gage Group

Chicago Athletic Club (1893, 1907, 1926)
12 South Michigan Avenue
Architects: Henry Ives Cobb, 1893; Schmidt, Garden
& Martin, 1907, 1926

Willoughby Tower (1929)
8 South Michigan Avenue
Architect: Samuel N. Cowen

Tower Building (1899, 1923)
6 North Michigan Avenue
Architects: Richard Schmidt, 1899; Holabird &
Roche, 1923

Ward Building (ca. 1885)
14 North Michigan Avenue
Architect: Unknown

10 Chicago Cultural Center

The idea of the cliff of buildings on Michigan Avenue facing Grant Park is so strongly associated with the imagery generated by Daniel Burnham for the 1909 Chicago Plan, that it is easy to forget that such an idea predates the Great Fire of 1871. Following the fire, when much of the debris was pushed into the lake to create the fill for what has become the park, much of the open space was converted to commercial use, especially rail yards for the Illinois Central. Despite the conflict between a shared public vision for the park and immediate private use of the land for rail traffic, architects designed the new buildings along the avenue as if they were in fact facing a large, public open space (the tracks were later hidden below ground level). The first building on Michigan Avenue to achieve the scale, quality, and character now associated with this view of the park came not from Burnham but Adler & Sullivan. Their magnificent Auditorium Building, and soon after its Annex (now the Congress Hotel), created a great gate at Michigan Avenue and Congress Parkway, the same central axis later defined by Burnham and now secured by Buckingham Fountain and Ivan Meštrović's mounted warriors. Further, as one scans the dates of the buildings along Michigan Avenue, it is apparent that many of them had been completed prior to the appearance of Burnham's plan, reinforcing the conclusion that here as elsewhere in his planning, the plan consolidated as much as innovated.

Like other ensembles that characterize Chicago, this one is not dominated by any single formal attribute beyond what one sees as an appropriate urban scale. Although one's memory might suggest uniform height or color or material, even a cursory analysis demonstrates that this unified effect derives more from the great scale—over a mile of frontage—than such other, in this case minor, elements. For most of these buildings, the principal facade faces the park, although these facades are often continued along their side street fronts. Many have their main entrances on the side street; for instance, to accommodate two distinct purposes the old Chicago Public Library (now Cultural Center) has a south entrance that leads to the former library space and a north entrance that leads to the rooms and great hall of the Grand Army of the Republic. For others, the importance of shop frontage on Michigan Avenue, as at the Railway Exchange, has pushed the main entry and corresponding orientation of the lobby, to the side.

The balance achieved between overall scale and variety of architectural forms does not mean that the individual buildings are polite background pieces. Certain associations are reinforced, as in the classical detail in the Cultural Center and Orchestra Hall. The classical motifs of such commercial structures as the Railway Exchange or People's Gas buildings suggest that some architects wished to continue these associations. However, the Gothic imagery in the University Club and Chicago Athletic Club permits other associations as well. Several buildings terminate in towers, but they do not share a single image. The most eclectic may also be the most sedate, as in the combination of a beehive-shaped blue glass lantern resting on four bison heads which in turn terminates a fine imitation of the Tomb of Mausolus at Halicarnassus at the Britannica Center. What unifies the group most effectively is the continuing shared view of scale that the architects displayed. Whether seen from the park, across the street, or right in front, these buildings present a rich visual experience that offers new detail and delight at every distance.

Blackstone Hotel (1909)   NR
636 South Michigan Avenue
Architects: Marshall & Fox

Combining dignity at its base, clarity in its shaft, and exu-
berance at its top, the Blackstone is among the liveliest of
the buildings along the Michigan Avenue cliff. Just to its
west along Balbo is the Blackstone Theater, built in 1911,
also designed by Marshall & Fox.

Congress Hotel (1893)
(Originally the Auditorium Annex)
504 South Michigan Avenue
Architects: Clinton J. Warren; Holabird &
  Roche (1902, 1907)

The architects of the Chicago school redefined the modern
hotel and apartment building as well as the office block,
and the Congress is the best and largest of the multiple-
dwelling structures. The vertical banks of projecting oriel
windows, a distinguishing feature of many Chicago hotels
and office buildings, allow the maximum admission of
light, at the same time imparting to the long street elevations a vigorous sense of rhythmic movement. The broad
openings of the base and the light screenlike walls clearly
suggest a thin curtain drawn over the columns and girders
of the steel frame. The original rough-faced granite blocks
of the first story and the shape of the paired windows in
the upper three stories indicate that Warren was deliber-
ately trying to harmonize the initial block of the hotel with
the Auditorium Building (3) immediately to the north. In
fact, Adler & Sullivan served Warren as consultants.

Auditorium Building (1889)   CL, NR
430 South Michigan Avenue
Architects: Adler & Sullivan

The Auditorium was Adler and Sullivan's first major commission, and its design and construction demonstrated Sullivan's developing genius and Adler's engineering skills. A complex structure meant to incorporate a grand theater, a hotel, and an office building presented complex engineering problems, which Adler successfully tackled. The immense weight of the load-bearing granite and limestone walls was unevenly distributed (being much greater beneath the tower on Congress Street), and Adler devised an ingenious foundation system to equalize settlement of the structure. Nevertheless, substantial settlement occurred, demonstrating the need for deep foundations under such heavy buildings. Alder also devised a complex system of interior iron framing that, among other things, carried the hotel kitchen and banquet hall on trusses above the stage and auditorium

space. For the theater, Adler devised a hydraulically operated stage and an early system of air conditioning. The
acoustics of the theater are superb, another product of Adler's genius. Sullivan designed a straightforward facade
whose powerful rhythm of simple geometric forms is based
on H. H. Richardson's design of the Marshall Field Wholesale Store (which stood until 1930 at Adams and Wells). On
the interior, especially in the theater, Sullivan's original ornament contributes to the grandeur of this monumental
civic structure. Other notable spaces of the former hotel include the lobby and stairwell, second-floor parlors and loggia, Ganz Hall, and the top-floor library, which occupies
the former dining room. The Auditorium flourished until
the 1930s. After a period of decline, it was purchased in
1946 by Roosevelt University. The theater itself remained in
disrepair until the 1960s, when the Auditorium Theater
Council undertook its restoration, reopening it in 1968.
Since the 1940s, architects associated with the restoration
have included Crombie Taylor, Harry Weese & Associates,
Skidmore, Owings & Merrill, and the Office of John Vinci.

4

Fine Arts Building (1885, 1896)   CL, NR
(Originally the Studebaker Building)
410 South Michigan Avenue
Architect: S. S. Beman

This building was long notable as a focus of Chicago's artistic life because of the cultural events that took place in it
and the artists who had studios there. As features of the
architectural composition, the two large columns in the
third and fourth stories seem incongruous in the design,
perhaps needing others to keep them company. The search
for variety in the shapes and groupings of the windows is
carried out along the same general lines as in the Auditorium (3) next door, but the result here suffers from compar-

ison with that more masterly design. Nonetheless, this is Beman's most exuberant elevation. In 1896, Beman raised the building from eight to ten stories and thoroughly renovated the interior when the building's focus changed from a carriage factory and showroom to an art-oriented rental building.

Chicago Club Building (1930)
81 East Van Buren Street
Architects: Granger & Bollenbacher

The Chicago Club formerly occupied a building on this
same site which had been designed by Burnham & Root
and built in 1887 as the home of the Art Institute of Chicago. After the Art Institute relocated to its present building in 1894, the Chicago Club occupied Burnham & Root's
Romanesque structure until 1929. The present fortresslike,
rugged Romanesque building is an appropriate bastion for
one of Chicago's exclusive private clubs. It also blends well
with its neighbors to the south, the Fine Arts Building (4)
and the Auditorium (3).

Railway Exchange Building (1904) NR

80 East Jackson Boulevard
Architects: D. H. Burnham & Company

The Railway Exchange was built to house the offices of several railroads at a time when Chicago was the rail center of the country. Burnham was not only the architect, but was also a major investor in the building and maintained his offices there for several years. The facade has an extremely delicate quality: its considerable glass area is articulated by

25

gleaming white terra-cotta molded into delicate ornament. The oriels project very slightly, creating a gentle rhythm along both street facades. The building is square in plan and has a central light well, the lower floors of which form a spacious lobby. The restoration, completed in 1985 by Frye, Gillian & Molinaro, concentrated on the lobby, including a marble floor and transparent skylights—one above the lobby, the other at the top of the building.

7

Orchestra Hall (1905)   NR
220 South Michigan Avenue
Architects: D. H. Burnham & Company;
    ninth-floor addition by Howard Van
    Doren Shaw (completed 1908); interior
    renovation by Harry Weese & Associates
    (completed 1966)

This neo-Georgian building reflects D. H. Burnham's growing interest in revival styles following the World's Columbian Exposition in 1893. The facade is of red brick complemented by limestone quoins, lintels, and other decorative features characteristic of the Georgian revival style. The tall windows of the second floor capped by Georgian fanlights reflect a high-ceilinged ballroom used for receptions and chamber concerts. The facade is topped by a classical cornice and a balustrade that hides a later ninth-floor addition. The auditorium space where the orchestra performs is at the west of the building and is four stories high. Above the fourth floor, the building is only one office space deep, creating a light court at the rear of the structure.

Orchestra Hall has been the home of the Chicago Symphony Orchestra for over eighty years. Organized by Theodore Thomas in 1891, the orchestra initially performed in Adler & Sullivan's Auditorium Theater. Thomas frequently complained that the Auditorium was too large and even threatened to quit as conductor before the Orchestral Association agreed to build a smaller hall. Burnham, as a trustee of the Orchestral Association, donated his design services. Within a few weeks after the orchestra first performed in the hall in December 1904, Thomas died. Burnham and others urged that the hall be named after the orchestra's founder and first conductor, so that the formal name of the building, "Theodore Thomas Orchestra Hall," is carved in stone above the entrance.

University Club (1909)
75 East Monroe Street
Architects: Holabird & Roche

Immediately to the north of the University Club are a pair of facades (part of the Gage Group [9]) that exemplify the stripped-down "Chicago frame," a form that draws attention to the structure of the building rather than to the historical ornament mounted prominently on earlier exteriors. The innovativeness of the device had brought fame to Chicago's commercial architecture during the 1890s and the early twentieth century. Yet by 1910 the firm that designed the Gage Group had invested its design of the University Club with Gothic detail—pointed arches, crenelations, finials, and the like—that reflected a widespread return in Chicago architecture to reliance on historical allusion.

Equally apparent, however, is the assurance with which the principal architect, Martin Roche, negotiated this later shift of objectives. The application of the Gothic style to the form of a tall modern building is expertly executed, and several of the major spaces of the interior are among the most magisterial rooms in the city. Chief among these are the great Cathedral Hall, based freely on London's fifteenth-century Crosby Hall and magnified by the stained-glass windows of Frederic Clay Bartlett. Bartlett also contributed the murals on the ceiling of the opulently panelled Michigan Room.

9

Gage Group (1898–99)   NR
18, 24, 30 South Michigan Avenue
Architects: Holabird & Roche; Louis H.
   Sullivan

Only the facade of the northernmost of these three buildings was designed by Sullivan. Note the fine relations established among piers, windows, and wall surfaces; the
excellence of proportions throughout; and the imaginative
use of original ornament. However, the architect designed
only an eight-story facade; the other four stories were
added in 1902. The two buildings to the south, 30 and 24
South Michigan, were done entirely by Holabird & Roche.
Their facades form an interesting contrast with that of
the north building. The basic design is the same, but they
do not have the refinement and elegance of proportion
and accent to be found in the Sullivan facade. The top
floor of 30 South Michigan was added in 1970 by Altman-
Saichek.

10

Chicago Cultural Center (1897)   CL, NR
78 East Washington Street
Architects: Shepley, Rutan & Coolidge (1897);
architects for restoration: Holabird &
    Root (1977)

From its completion in 1897 until 1974, the structure now
known as the Chicago Cultural Center housed the central
operations of the Chicago Public Library. By the later 1960s
it had become evident that the central library collections
and the functions of the library system had outgrown the
building. The board of directors studied the problem and
decided to renovate the building as a popular library and a
center for cultural activities, with the idea of constructing a
new building to house most of the collection. With the
completion of the new Harold Washington Library Center
(27), the use of this building is again being studied.

The building entrances are on the north and south
sides, each serving a different area of the building. The exterior design and elements of the interior are derived from
Italian Renaissance precedents. Many walls are wainscoted

with wood or marble; some are paneled for their entire height in marble. The floors are covered with mosaic tile. The Washington Street entrance to the former library uses the Ionic order. The entry hall contains a grand staircase of white Carrara marble. The balustrades are inlaid with intricate mosaics designed in the Tiffany style and composed of marble and glass around medallions of dark green Irish marble.

The third floor adjoining the grand staircase is a civic reception center which houses an illuminated stained-glass Tiffany dome. The design of the fourth floor, where the Exhibition Hall is located, is based on several Italian Renaissance palaces. The Randolph Street entrance uses the Doric order to announce its purpose as the entrance to the rooms of the Grand Army of the Republic. A subdued and quiet staircase leads to the second-floor Memorial Hall and small theater—both refurbished while retaining the original Tiffany stained-glass dome and remarkably well-preserved wall fixtures. An addition has been built along

Garland Court, filling in the U-shape and enabling people to cross from the north to the south side on all floors, which had not previously been possible. The addition encloses a garden court.

11

Carbide and Carbon Building (1929)
230 North Michigan Avenue
Architects: Burnham Brothers

The color contrasts of the forty-story Carbide and Carbon Building make it unique among Chicago's Art Deco skyscrapers. Although many of New York's Art Deco buildings employ deep-toned polychromatic materials, those in Chicago tend to be light gray Bedford limestone with, when present, light metal spandrel panels. The base of the

Carbide and Carbon Building is sheathed in black polished granite with black marble and bronze trim at the entrance. The tower is clad in dark green terra-cotta, and the pinnacle is trimmed in gold terra-cotta. The finial-like forms at the top of the building are also characteristic of the Art Deco skyscrapers of New York.

Despite these elements, its basic massing—a relatively small tower atop a more substantial base—relates it to a large number of Chicago skyscrapers of the 1920s.

Amoco Building and Plaza (1974)
200 East Randolph Street
Architects: Edward Durell Stone and the
  Perkins & Will Partnership

This is the giant building Chicagoans love to hate. Because of the decline in the reputation of its architect, its absence of corner offices, and the replacement of the original marble cladding with the present granite, it is the subject of a rich local folklore. For his part, Stone seems to have adopted Louis Sullivan's idea of the tall office building— that it should be "a proud and soaring thing, rising in sheer exultation . . . from bottom to top . . . without a single dissenting line."

In its relatively open site, it offers spectacular views of the city and the lake from even the lowest floors.

This slender steel structure faced with light gray granite is the corporate headquarters of the Amoco Oil Company. The triangular sections of granite contain the bulk of mechanical services such as the utilities and air conditioning, thus permitting flush window walls inside the building.

The tower faces Grant Park, where it rises above street level to a height of 1,136 feet. A delightful lower-level plaza contains a fascinating reflecting pool and "sounding" sculpture by Harry Bertoia that consists of eleven separate units, each composed of tall clusters of hard copper alloy rods welded to a naval brass plate and mounted on 18-inch pedestals of black granite. A light breeze starts the rods' movement, which in turn produces swishing sounds.

Art Institute of Chicago (1893)
Michigan Avenue at Adams Street
Architects: Shepley, Rutan & Coolidge, and
   others

Additions:
Gunsaulus Hall (1916) Shepley, Rutan & Coolidge
Hutchinson Wing and McKinlock Court (1924) Coolidge &
   Hodgson
Goodman Theater (1925) Howard van Doren Shaw
Ferguson Wing (1958) Holabird, Root & Burgee
Morton Wing (1962) Shaw, Metz Associates
South Garden (1965) Dan Kiley
East Wing (1976) Skidmore, Owings & Merrill
Stock Exchange Arch and Trading Room (1977) Vinci/
   Kenny
Original Building Galleries Renovated (1987) Skidmore,
   Owings & Merrill
Main Entry and Lobby Restored (1987) Office of John Vinci
Rice Building (1988) Hammond, Beeby & Babka
North Garden (1991) Hanna/Olin

The Art Institute is the oldest home of the visual arts in
Chicago. In 1887 Burnham & Root designed and built the
first Art Institute building at the southwest corner of Michigan Avenue and Van Buren Street, inspired by the example of the great Boston architect H. H. Richardson.
However, when Richardson's successors, Shepley, Rutan &
Coolidge received the commission for the 1893 building,
their classically inspired design signalled a shift in style
from the Richardsonian Romanesque of their late master
and of Burnham & Root's 1887 Art Institute.

   The original building, now called the Allerton Building, opened in December 1893 as an art museum after its
initial use as an auxiliary space for the 1893 World's Columbian Exposition. It is the first major Chicago building
to take the classical forms and light colors of that fair and
put them to use in a permanent building.

The small lobby leads to the large central stair hall. Unlike the vast halls and rotundas of some museums, this directness suggests the highly commercial character of the city—visitors wish to get to the goods quickly, not loiter in the foyer.

The renovation of the second-floor galleries of the Allerton Building restored the inner circulation corridor, with large, top-lighted galleries on the perimeter. The ample natural and artificial light in the large galleries is excellent for paintings, while the more intimate scale and carefully controlled artificial light in the corridor permits the exhibition of fragile works on paper related to the larger works in the main galleries.

McKinlock Court is a pleasant oasis where lunch is served in the open air in summer. The classical arcades of the court are a pleasant foil to the *Fountain of the Tritons*, by Carl Milles. Just to the north of McKinlock Court is Howard van Doren Shaw's fine Goodman Theater.

The East Wing, containing galleries, an auditorium, dining and meeting spaces, other services, and the School of the Art Institute, is aggressively angular in its demonstration of the geometrically based field theory of its architect,

Walter Netsch of Skidmore, Owings & Merrill. The high-ceilinged Trading Room of Adler & Sullivan's Stock Exchange (demolished in 1972) was incorporated in the new construction, and the entry arch of the destroyed masterpiece was reerected in a new garden outside the East Wing. Isamu Noguchi's sculpture fountain designed for the American bicentennial is here as well.

14

Grant Park Museum Complex
Lake Shore Drive at East Roosevelt Road

Field Museum of Natural History (1912)   NR
Lake Shore Drive and East Roosevelt Road
Architects: D. H. Burnham & Company
    (until 1912); Graham, Burnham &
    Company (1912–17); Graham,
    Anderson, Probst & White (1917–20);
    renovation by Harry Weese & Associates
    (1978)

John G. Shedd Aquarium (1929, 1991)
Lake Shore Drive and East Roosevelt Road
Architects: Graham, Anderson, Probst &
    White (1929); Lohan Associates (1991)

Max Adler Planetarium (1930, 1973)
East End of Solidarity Drive
Architects: Ernest Grunsfeld (1930); C. F.
   Murphy & Associates (1973)

Chicago's cultural institutions have traditionally been built
close to each other and to the downtown center. In the
seven blocks along Michigan Avenue that separate the Auditorium Building (3) from the Cultural Center (formerly
the Public Library, 10) are the Fine Arts Building (4), Orchestra Hall (7), and the Art Institute (13).

A second major complex, more dramatically sited and
made up of the Field Museum of Natural History, the
Shedd Aquarium, and the Adler Planetarium, is somewhat
distant from the first in both space and time, though not by
much in either dimension. While each of the buildings in
this ensemble was designed independently, together they
form a remarkably harmonious cluster at the south end of
Chicago Harbor.

If one adds a fourth structure nearby, Soldier Field
(140), a sports stadium built in 1925, the group provides an
exceptional architectural experience. Northbound Lake
Shore Drive passes Soldier Field and the Field Museum on
one side, the Adler Planetarium and the Shedd Aquarium
on the other—where a splendid view of downtown unfolds.

The prevailingly classical mode of the complex is most apparent in the Ionic order of the Field Museum, the Doric of the Shedd Aquarium and Soldier Field, and even in the central plan and domical structure of the Adler Planetarium, whose ancient Roman devices are not disguised by its Art Deco ornament.

A distinctly modernist note is struck in the glass façade of the Oceanarium, a recent addition to the Shedd Aquarium that is large enough to accommodate whales, dolphins, seals, sea otters, and penguins. It is sited low enough on the lake side of the aquarium not to interrupt the profile of the older building.

Although Daniel Burnham died in 1912, seven years before the first of these buildings was opened to the public in completed form, his influence in their design and siting is too great to be ignored. He himself began work on the Field Museum as early as 1902, and its present location corresponds with the place he assigned a comparably imposing civic building in his Chicago Plan of 1909. Northerly Island, site of the planetarium, was one of the areas of landfill also conceived in Burnham's plan. The Grant Park complex has been called by historian Carl Condit "architecturally the most impressive 'cultural center' in the United States."

Efforts are underway to make it more arresting still. The Museum Campus Plan was conceived in the late 1980s as part of a proposed 1992 worlds fair in Chicago. The fair was never realized, but the plan remains intact. It would move the northbound lanes of Lake Shore Drive westward so that they would run immediately adjacent to the present southbound lanes. The area thus freed of vehicular traffic would be landscaped, producing an even more perceptible integration among the several buildings in it.

Union Loop Elevated (1897)
Chief Engineer: John Waddell

Although downtown Chicago has been called the Loop
since the cable car days of the 1880s, it is the century-long
presence of the Loop Elevated structure that has reinforced
the name and kept it current. Developed to rationalize the
confusion of rapid transit lines that had been built to serve
the needs of Loop workers, the Loop Elevated at first
joined four separate systems into one single central system.
Organized by Charles Tyson Yerkes, the design and construction of the system by Waddell was published as the definitive solution to the problem. In recent years, two Loop
stations have been rebuilt. At Quincy and Wells, the station
has been restored to its 1897 appearance, while at Adams
and Wabash, the station has been rebuilt with contemporary materials, especially in the use of large glass sheets
providing a view of the facade of the Art Institute.

Wieboldt's Annex (1900, 1905)
(Originally Mandel Brothers Annex)
Northwest corner of Wabash Avenue and
    Madison Street
Architects: Holabird & Roche

This distinguished building compares favorably with Sullivan's masterpiece, the Carson Pirie Scott Store (24). Wide
window bays and narrow piers contribute to the openness
of the facade, and continuous projecting bands of ornament
at the sill level of the windows emphasize the strong horizontality. The nine-story south half was built in 1900. In
1905 the eleven-story north half and two additional stories
on the south half were built.

Jewelers' Building (1882)   CL, NR
15–19 South Wabash
Architect: Dankmar Adler

Designed and built while Louis Sullivan was working as a designer-draftsman in Adler's independent practice, the Jewelers' Building is similar to the commercial buildings constructed in downtown Chicago after the Fire of 1871. The Jewelers' Building emphasizes the openness of its facade and demonstrates the quality of early Sullivan ornament. The Egyptoid and Neo-Grec elements of the facade and parapet reflect Sullivan's experience in the office of Philadelphia architect Frank Furness. The ground floor has been completely remodeled, but some trace of its original ornament survives in the single pier on the north (alley) side of the structure. Compare the pressed brick and green terra-cotta Silversmith Building of 1897 by D. H. Burnham & Company across the street at 10 South Wabash. At 18–24, Sullivan designed the new shop fronts of the first two floors in 1896.

Chapin and Gore Building (1904)   CL, NR
(Later the Nepeennauk Building, now
   the 63 East Adams Building)
63 East Adams Street
Architect: Richard E. Schmidt

There is an originality almost mannerist here, as in the split
window-framing panels on the second floor, contrasting
with the beautifully simple piers above. "Upside-down capitals," as they were called, once flowered at the top of the
piers. The original cornice has been replaced with a parapet, and this, with the absence of the original capitals,
makes the upper part of the building incongruously bare in
relation to the lower part. Overall, the elegance and sophistication of the handling of the brick in the facade indicates
the quality of Hugh Garden's design. Garden subsequently
became Schmidt's partner.

McClurg Building (1900) NR
218 South Wabash Avenue
Architects: Holabird & Roche

The light and open character of the facade is remarkable.
Compare the relative emphasis on the horizontal versus the
vertical and on openness versus solidity in the treatment of
the wall of this building and those of the Marquette Building (33) and the Carson Pirie Scott Store (24). The three
buildings also offer interesting comparisons of the treatment of the "Chicago window," that is, a window in which
a fixed center light is flanked by movable sashes at the
sides.

At night, the light cast from the offices onto the fluted
piers of the facade reveals qualities of light and shade not
always associated with such forms.

Loop End Building   (1872)   CL, NR
(Formerly Page Brothers)
Southeast corner of State and Lake streets
Architect: John Mills Van Osdel

John Mills Van Osdel was the first architect to practice in
Chicago, and the Lake Street facade of this building is one
of only two cast-iron fronts in downtown Chicago (the
other is at 17 West Adams). A cast-iron front consists of
prefabricated, often finely detailed, cast-iron panels that are
affixed to an otherwise traditional building which has load-
bearing side walls and interior columns. Cast-iron fronts,
which open a substantial surface area for windows, were
common in New York beginning in 1842, and the earliest
ones in Chicago were designed by Van Osdel in 1856. They
lost popularity within a few years after the Fire of 1871.

After State Street replaced Lake Street as Chicago's
major retail thoroughfare, the State Street facade of this
building, which had been a simple load-bearing masonry
wall, was remodeled to become the major facade. This facade and an additional story were done by Hill & Wolters-
dorf in 1902. The building has been rehabilitated as part of
the restoration of the Chicago Theater (21).

Chicago Theater (1921)   CL
175 North State Street
Architects: C. W. & George L. Rapp

Designed by a firm noted for its theaters, the Chicago is an
early example of the lavish movie palaces of the 1920s
where fantasy and illusion were not restricted to the screen
but extended to the architectural surroundings as well. The
State Street facade, partially obscured by a later marquee
and six-story vertical sign, is organized on a triumphal arch
motif; the off-white terra-cotta sheathing is molded into
neobaroque ornamental forms. The interior follows the
precedent of French Second Empire style designs which revived baroque forms to create an effect of overwhelming
grandeur. Although the inner lobby has unfortunately been
remodeled, most of the original ornament remains intact.

Marshall Field and Company Store　　　NR
(1892, 1902, 1906, 1907, 1914)
Block bounded by Wabash Avenue and
    State Street, and Washington and
    Randolph streets
Architects: D. H. Burnham & Company

This enormous structure houses one of the world's best-
known department stores. The earliest section of the present store is the heavily rusticated Renaissance palazzo-like
edifice at the northwest corner of Wabash and Washington.
This was built in 1892 as an annex to an 1879 structure occupied by Field's at the northeast corner of State and Washington. The north half of the State Street front was next

completed in 1902, and then the middle section of the Wabash Avenue front in 1906. The original 1879 building was demolished and replaced by the present south half of the State Street front in 1907. Finally, the north section of the Wabash Avenue front was completed in 1914. The design of the four later sections is commercial in function, classical in inspiration. It consists of a three-story base, a seven-story central section topped by an entablature, and a two-story columned top with a classical cornice. The main entrance on State Street has a high portico with four Ionic columns resting on bases and topped by an entablature and a carved balustrade. Perhaps the most familiar exterior features are the elaborate clocks at the corners of the State Street facade. On the interior, a light court in the southwest section features a dome designed by Louis Comfort Tiffany. The Field Store is the prototype of other large urban department stores that Burnham designed for Selfridge's in London (1906; Selfridge was a former Field partner); Gimbel's in New York (1909); Wanamaker's in Philadelphia (1909); the May Company in Cleveland (1912); and Filene's in Boston (1912).

While the later sections show Burnham's most severe trabeation, the 1893 section, designed by Charles Atwood, with its heavily rusticated stone and round arches, recalls Richardson's Marshall Field Wholesale Store. Here the retail is more elegant and refined, but one should have no doubt of the relation of the wholesale and retail aspects of the enterprise.

23

Reliance Building (1895)   CL, NR
36 North State Street
Architects: D. H. Burnham & Company

The Reliance was a remarkably advanced structure for its time. Once the skeletal frame relieved the exterior walls of carrying even their own weight, buildings could be sheathed almost entirely in glass. No building of its day came closer to this than the Reliance. Slender piers and mullions and narrow spandrels, all of cream-colored terracotta, and broad windows contribute to the openness of the facade. The strength and convenience of steel construction were shown in the piecemeal manner in which the building was constructed. In 1890 John Root designed a sixteen-story building for this site, but only the foundations and first story were built at that time. These were "slipped under"

the upper stories of a four-story, heavy masonry building already there, these upper stories continuing in use during construction. In 1894 the older stories were "knocked off" and the present building carried on up. The designer in charge in 1894–95 was Charles Atwood of D. H. Burnham & Company, who designed the frame and enclosure of the new tower.

Generations of observers have learned to see the audacity of this building despite the tawdriness of its current condition. Plans to restore the building have been developed, but at this time, no sure steps have been taken.

24

Carson Pirie Scott and Company Store   CL, NR
(1899, 1903–4)
(Originally the Schlesinger and Mayer Store)
State and Madison streets (SE corner)
Architect: Louis H. Sullivan

The easternmost section of three bays on Madison Street was built first, and the main section, extending around the corner and with seven bays on State Street, several years later. (The third section was done by D. H. Burnham & Company in 1906, and the southernmost by Holabird & Root in 1960–61.) The wide windows and narrow piers express the steel frame, but the details suggest the sensitive designer above all. The fine proportions of the window openings, the firm emphasis in the moldings around them, the accent given by the line of delicate ornament on the horizontal wall sections, all contribute to a perfection of design rarely to be found. The rich ornament of the first and second floors demonstrates Sullivan's idea that the display windows were like pictures and deserved rich frames, and his prophetic power is seen in this, if one compares old photographs showing the stodgy displays of the time with window-dressers' art of today. The ornament has been returned to its original reddish-green color after years of

being painted gray. Sullivan intended the ornament to resemble oxidized bronze, an effect achieved by applying a
coat of brownish-red paint and then applying a layer of
deep green paint in such a way that the undercoat of red
shows through in places. Other features of the original design have also been restored. A ceiling that had been added
later was removed from the rotunda entrance, revealing the
original column capitals. The glass panels on the outside
and inside of the rotunda have been opened up so that nat-

ural light is admitted to the store. Chicago architect John Vinci was responsible for the renovation in 1979.

As in many of the older buildings, the original projection, or cornice, at the top has been replaced by a bald parapet. The large festoons of ornament which were originally set outside the piers between the first and second floors have also been removed. (One wonders whether they could ever have seemed very closely related to the wall, rather than "hung on" it.) They contained the initials "SM" for the owners. The architect's initials "LHS" can still be seen in some of the ornament, perhaps slipped in by George G. Elmslie, who, as Sullivan's chief designer, carried out much of the ornamental design.

Chicago Building (1904)   NR

7 West Madison Street

Architects: Holabird & Roche

The Chicago Building is another of the high-quality designs produced by the prolific firm of Holabird & Roche. Continuous vertical piers emphasize the height of the narrow State Street facade. This verticality is repeated in the projecting bays along Madison Street that alternate with wide windows to create a rhythm that carries the longer facade. The corner piers are emphasized as in the firm's earlier Marquette Building. The top and bottom floors are set off from the intervening floors, also recalling the design of the Marquette. The Chicago Building is one of the few downtown structures that has its original cornice intact, although today the building's original reddish-brown brick and terra-cotta sheathing are blackened by grime.

26

Second Leiter Building (1891) NR
State and Van Buren streets (SE corner)
Architects: Jenney & Mundie

This building is an example of the "commercial style" for which Chicago was famous. The piers are narrow enough to suggest the metal frame within them, as do the slender piers and high ceilings of the interior. Ornament is sparse, economy is suggested, and the general effect is simple and direct. In using pilaster strips to organize the facade, Jenney continued to exploit the hierarchy that the use of orders implied. The powerful stability this decision produces can best be seen today from one of the upper floors of the new Harold Washington Library (27).

Harold Washington Library Center (1991)
Bounded by Van Buren, State, Congress
   streets, and Plymouth Court
Architects: Hammond, Beeby & Babka

Much of the heavy publicity preceding the 1991 opening of
this, the new main Chicago Public Library, stemmed from
two sources: a long-lasting argument over where the new
structure should be erected (indeed, should it be a new
building at all, or a rehabilitated old one?), and the formal
competition for a final design that unfolded once a site was
selected, just south of the Loop.

Nonetheless, the winning entry generated considerable
controversy in its own right. Chief architect Thomas Beeby
conceived a building of the sort one rightly calls an edifice,
which for the most part looks as if the modernist revolution
of the last 75 years had never happened. Clad mostly in

masonry, with granite on the lower levels and brick above, it is monumental in more than its scale, harking back to the Beaux-Arts manner of the late nineteenth century not only in its powerful axial symmetry but in the heavy representational decoration that graces its exterior. It is clearly indebted to the ancient Western tradition of grandiloquent civic monuments.

Yet a closer look confirms that it is a contemporary building after all, especially in its self-consciously neo-mannerist mixture of old and new elements. The whole west wall and the pedimental attic are clad in glass and steel components whose modernist look is counterposed violently but knowingly with the building's overall muscular classicism. The granite base and the attic house the public areas of the library, the most imposing part of which is the glass-roofed winter garden on the top story. The less differentiated stack spaces of the middle floors are expressed on the facade by tall, deeply incised arched windows that reinforce the dignity and weight of the whole. Other latter-day touches may be found in the decorative program of the interior, which features sculpture and painting by well-known artists from Chicago and elsewhere.

Delaware Building (1874)   CL, NR
36 West Randolph Street
Architects: Wheelock & Thomas

The Delaware is a large commercial structure built in
downtown Chicago shortly after the Great Fire of 1871. Begun in 1872 as a five-story building, its complex facade with
variform window openings, deep moldings, and extensive
ornament is typical of the High Victorian Italianate style
popular at the time. The Delaware Building originally had
five stories above an English basement and extended farther
east along Randolph. The first two floors were of iron and
glass to provide wide display windows for shops; the upper
floors contained offices and did not require such wide windows. In 1889, the first two floors were remodeled; three
additional floors and an atrium were added. Inside, the
sky-lighted atrium lobby remains largely intact. The building was restored in 1976 by Wilbert Hasbrouck.

Richard J. Daley Center (1965)
(Originally Civic Center)
Block bounded by Washington, Randolph,
Dearborn, and Clark streets
Architects: C. F. Murphy Associates; Loebl,
    Schlossman & Bennett; Skidmore, Owings
    & Merrill

The structural bays of this 31-story, 650-foot building are tremendously large: an unprecedented 87 feet long and almost 48 feet wide. The 42-foot bays of the CNA building at 55 East Jackson Street had been designer Jacques Brownson's first use of such scale. The perimeter columns, spandrels, and mullions are of self-weathering Cor-ten steel that over the years has turned a deep russet color; windows are amber glass. Note that the cruciform columns become narrower as they rise higher, reflecting the greater weight of the frame at the base and the minimum weight at the top. The architects have exploited the Miesian idiom with verve and finesse.

The building houses courtrooms and offices, and is sited at the northern part of the block to allow for a large plaza intended for civic functions and public use. A sculpture executed in Cor-ten steel from a design given to the city by Pablo Picasso dominates the plaza. The building and its plaza were renamed after the death of the late Mayor Richard J. Daley.

The high ceilings in this building give the corridors a sense of spaciousness and grandeur associated with public buildings but not often with modern architecture.

30

Brunswick Building (1965)
69 West Washington Street
Architects: Skidmore, Owings & Merrill

Unlike most of its contemporary neighbors, the 38-story Brunswick Building employs load-bearing exterior walls. Because the building loads are supported by these concrete screen walls and by a shear-wall core, the interior spaces are column-free. At the base, loads are transferred from the screen wall to ten perimeter columns by means of an enormous (1½-story) transfer girder. This creates an openness at the ground floor that would not have existed had the screen wall been carried to grade level. A slight inward curve above the base provides a transition between the massive girder and the open screen wall above it. Unfortunately, the ground-floor piers are sheathed in travertine and the girder in high-density paneled concrete, materials that do not harmonize with the screen wall and consequently detract from the design.

Inland Steel Building (1957)
30 West Monroe Street
Architects: Skidmore, Owings & Merrill

The first tall building to go up in the Loop since the
Depression, Inland Steel is among the most beautiful dem-
onstrations of modernist architectural theory. Service and
vertical circulation are placed in the opaque, nearly square
tower on the eastern edge of the site. This permits open
column-free space on the office floors in the stainless steel
and blue-green glass rectangular tower on the west side of
the site. The supporting columns have been placed outside
the curtain wall, giving a forceful vertical emphasis.

First National Bank Building (1969)

Madison Street between Dearborn and
   Clark streets
Architects: C. F. Murphy Associates; the
   Perkins & Will Partnership

The most conspicuous feature of this 850-foot-high building is the inward-sweeping curve of the columns that stand
outside the long elevations. The choice of the shape arises
from sound functional planning. The maximum floor area
is required at the street and mezzanine levels, where commercial banking facilities serve the heaviest public traffic.
Above the base other banking activities dictated a smaller

but still extensive floor area. The space above, which is rented to tenants, meets their needs for perimeter offices and less floor area. At the very top of the building a longitudinal row of separate penthouses encloses various mechanical and electrical utilities. Elevator shafts, stairs, main ducts, and pipes are housed in utility cores placed at both ends of the building to allow maximum open banking space.

This hierarchical arrangement of functions, as one of the designing architects called it, compelled a marked deviation from the standard prismatic form of the skyscraper. A tapering envelope would provide maximum resistance to the horizontal forces of wind, but an upward-curving one would preserve the structural and functional validity while achieving the most graceful form. The steel framing members of the bank building are sheathed in gray-speckled granite, harmonizing nicely with the bronze-tinted glass. The powerfully articulated walls stand squarely in the Chicago tradition.

Of the three public plazas developed along Dearborn Street in the 1960s, the multilevel plaza here, with a large mosaic by Marc Chagall, fountains, outdoor cafe, and summertime entertainment, is by far the most successful.

33

Marquette Building (1894)   CL, NR
140 South Dearborn Street
Architects: Holabird & Roche

In the Marquette, Holabird & Roche gave forceful aesthetic expression to the skeleton frame and developed the basic pattern that would characterize their work for the next thirty years. This pattern consists of strong, continuous projecting piers and less forceful, recessed spandrels framing wide Chicago windows to create a cellular facade that expresses the geometry of the supporting frame. The treatment of the top and bottom follows Sullivan's idea of setting these stories off from the others. The building was originally topped by a cornice which was later removed and replaced by the present unsightly top floor. The bay at the western end of the Adams Street facade is also a later addition. Brilliant mosaics in the lobby and bronze reliefs above the entrance depict incidents in the life of Père Marquette, an early explorer of this area. The artists include Hermon MacNeil, Edward Kemeys, Amy Bradley, and J. A. Holzer. After a period when its existence was threatened by developers, the Marquette underwent extensive renovation in 1978 by Holabird & Root.

34

Federal Center   (1964, 1975, 1991)
Dearborn Street between Jackson Boulevard
   and Adams Street
Architects: Schmidt, Garden & Erikson;
   Mies van der Rohe; C. F. Murphy
   Associates; A. Epstein & Sons (1964,
   1975); Fujikawa, Johnson (1991)

One of the finest works of Ludwig Mies van der Rohe, this
complex is interesting, not only for the individual buildings, but for their relationship to each other in a masterful
composition around a central plaza. On the east side of
Dearborn Street is the 30-story Dirksen courthouse and office building, the first of the group to be built. The block to
the west is occupied at its southern end by the 45-story
Kluczynski office building and at the northwestern corner
by a single-story post office whose lofty ceiling relates to the
lobbies of the two towers. Almost one-half of the total site
is plaza. The major plaza space opens to the north, where
its edge is defined by Holabird and Roche's 1894 Marquette

Building (33). At the inner corner of the plaza is Alexander Calder's red-painted, spontaneous free-form stabile *Flamingo*, which stands in perfect contrast to the disciplined sophistication of the dark steel and glass curtain walls.

The Federal Center is the southernmost of the three major plazas along Dearborn Street that contain large-scale works of contemporary art.

The spareness of the plaza's elements, unlike that at the First National Bank Plaza, does not invite strollers or crowds at lunchtime. However, it is the central forum for symbolic expression as people from all points of view use the space to petition the government.

The Metcalf building was added to the Federal Center in 1991 to the southwest along Clark Street between Jackson and Van Buren streets.

35

William J. Campbell United States Courthouse Annex (1975)
(Metropolitan Detention Center)
Van Buren Street between Clark and
   Federal streets
Architects: Harry Weese & Associates

Located just a block away from the U.S. District Courthouse, the Metropolitan Detention Center was built to accommodate persons awaiting trial and testifying at trials as well as other short-term detainees. The triangular shape of the building allows maximum perimeter space so that each inmate's room can have a 5-inch-wide window (the maximum allowed without bars by the Bureau of Prisons); window openings are splayed outward to allow a better view. The triangular shape also minimizes interior corridor space that requires surveillance. Stairwells and elevator cores are located in the corners.

The lower eleven floors contain administrative and medical facilities and mechanical equipment. The upper floors are divided into two-story self-contained units with inmates' rooms arranged around common lounge, dining, and visitors' areas. The roof houses a walled, landscaped exercise yard. Exposed reinforced concrete and articulated construction joints underscore the essentially utilitarian design of this dramatic structure. The site also accommodates a 7-story garage to the south and a triangular landscaped plaza to the northeast.

Monadnock Building (1891)   CL, NR

53 West Jackson Boulevard
Architects: Burnham & Root; south half,
    Holabird & Roche (1893)

This, observed nineteenth century architectural critic Montgomery Schuyler, may be "the thing itself," thus initiating its reputation as a masterpiece of bold simplicity. The slab-like form of the Monadnock, a geological term indicating a mountain which is freestanding and surrounded by a plain, emerges square at grade. The 6-foot-thick wall then curves

in slightly at the second story and out at its summit, in a subtle echo of the Egyptian pylon. Even more exciting are the rippling bays of the north half of the building, which contrast handsomely with the more prismatic bays of the south half.

Using four sections in order to serve the interests of the developers better, Burnham & Root established the overall plan and built the northern two sections using bearing wall construction, which accounts, in part, for its distinctive expression. Holabird & Roche designed the southern two sections, expressing them as a metal frame, although the recent restoration of the building has shown that even the northern half of this work uses outer bearing walls. Originally each section had its own name, taken from a New England mountain. From north to south it was Monadnock, Kearsarge (both in New Hampshire), Wachusetts (in Massachusetts), and Katahdin (in Maine).

37

Fisher Building (1896)   CL, NR
343 South Dearborn Street
Architects: D. H. Burnham & Company

This is an early example of the application of Gothic style to the skyscraper, an ornamental scheme that would become popular briefly during the 1920s. The detail is consistently Gothic in inspiration, there are frequent visual puns on the building's name, and the corner piers are even given a Gothic form with engaged colonnettes (or moldings). One may note the emphasis on height which this accomplishes, aided here by the verticals of the projecting bays. The design achieves a notable openness and lightness, hardly inferior to the Reliance Building, and thus vigorously expresses the steel frame enlivened by the presence of the historical detail.

38

Old Colony Building (1894)   CL, NR
407 South Dearborn Street
Architects: Holabird & Roche

The Old Colony is the last remaining downtown building
with rounded projecting corner bays, a device often employed by Holabird & Roche and other architects to create
highly desirable corner spaces on the interior and an interesting silhouette on the exterior. Note that continuous vertical piers along Dearborn Street balance the breadth of that
facade, while continuous horizontal spandrels along Van
Buren Street emphasize the width of the narrow facade.
The Old Colony was the first structure to employ a system
of portal arches to brace it against wind loads, an innovative
solution to a basic problem of tall skeleton-framed buildings. Portal bracing had long been employed in bridge con-

struction and had been introduced into the construction of skyscrapers in the early 1890s, although not in the arched form used here.

Manhattan Building (1891)   CL, NR
431 South Dearborn Street
Architect: William LeBaron Jenney

The structural advances that led to the development of the Chicago school contributed to the emergence of a dichotomy between the role of architect and that of engineer. Jenney was primarily an engineer, and the Manhattan Building represents an important engineering accomplishment. This building and Burnham & Root's Rand McNally

Building (now demolished) were the first tall office buildings to use skeleton construction throughout. Even the party walls were carried by the metal frame, in this case on beams cantilevered out, that is, extending beyond their supporting columns. The building thus displays Jenney's interest in structural matters and his inventiveness in using the new structural material, either iron or steel. If Jenney's nearly contemporary Second Leiter Building (26) displays the discipline of a single hierarchical idea, the Manhattan seems to take pleasure in presenting itself as an assemblage of the possibilities for solving the facade of the tall metal-framed building. Particularly fetching are the faces in the trumps of the bays. Hasbrouck-Hunderman converted the building to residential use in their 1982 renovations.

Printers' Row

40 Dearborn Street Station

41 731 South Plymouth Building

New Franklin Building (1912)
718–736 South Dearborn Street
Architect: George C. Nimmons

Donohue and Henneberry Building (1883)
701–723 South Dearborn Street
Architect: Julius Speyer

Donohue and Henneberry Annex (1913)
725–733 South Dearborn Street
Architect: Alfred S. Alschuler

Transportation Building (1911)
608 South Dearborn Street
Architect: William Strippelman

42 Pontiac Building

Terminals Building (1892)
537 South Dearborn Street
Architect: John Mills Van Osdel

Duplicator Building (1886)
530 South Dearborn Street
Architect: Unknown

Franklin Building (1888)
519–531 South Dearborn Street
Architects: Baumann & Lotz

Morton Building (1896)
508 South Dearborn Street
Architects: Jenney & Mundie

The three blocks of Dearborn Street south from Congress to the tower of the Dearborn Street Station, which gives the district its focus, were developed over three decades, from the 1880s to the 1920s. High-speed presses and efficient rail distribution of their products led many printing and publishing businesses to concentrate in this area. The powerful frames and freight elevators of the buildings, along with efficient use of natural and artificial lighting permitted the vertical integration of all printing tasks within the same structure. Typically, the presses were placed in the basement, independent commercial shops faced the streets on the first floor, and the printing concern's other tasks—binding, shipping, administration—occupied the upper floors. Often space on the upper floors was rented to others in the trade.

Chicago's printing industry was very competitive and a national center of the graphic arts. As a result of this and because these buildings face the path between an important rail passenger station and the commercial center in the Loop, many of the facades received more attention and finer materials than structures for similar purposes on less prominent sites. These facades tended to reflect current architectural tastes—whether the Richardson-influenced Donohue and Henneberry Building, the Chicago school exemplar Pontiac Building, or the richly and persuasively eclectic Lakeside Press Building, where Shaw developed images and motifs illustrating the history and character of printing. Chicago artist Oskar Gross designed the tile mosaics on Nimmons's New Franklin Building. Regardless of the materials used or the architectural tradition being recalled or developed, the facades are clearly and powerfully articulated, and in studying the proportions of window and wall, the architects most often gave preference to the open spaces of the windows.

After the Second World War, the printing industry changed considerably. As technology became more sophisticated, smaller printing companies were put out of business or consolidated into larger companies that could afford modern equipment; the railroads became less important as a means of transporting printed products; and auxiliary services previously performed by smaller companies were incorporated into larger printing operations. As the printing industry became less centralized, South Dearborn Street lost its identity as Printers' Row. Beginning in the late 1970s many of the structures were converted to residential use.

40

Dearborn Street Station   (1885)   CL, NR
South Dearborn Street at West Polk Street
Architect: Cyrus L. W. Eidlitz

This is Chicago's only surviving late nineteenth-century passenger station. The basic composition of the Romanesque structure remains intact, although the building was greatly altered after a fire in 1922. The tall clock tower serves like an obelisk to announce the station along the Dearborn Street vista. Walls are of red pressed brick atop a base of rusticated pink granite and are ornamented by details of red terra-cotta. Prior to the 1922 fire, the building was crowned by a variety of steeply pitched roofs with dormers. The present third story of the central block is a later addition. The building has not functioned as a passenger station since 1971 and its train shed was demolished in 1976.

The 1986 adaptive reuse, intended to serve the commercial needs of the residents of the newly developed Dearborn Park neighborhood, has yet to be successful. Architects for this were Kaplan, McLaughlin/Diaz, and Hasbrouck & Hunderman.

41

731 South Plymouth Building   NR
(1897, 1901)
(Originally the Lakeside Press Building)
731 South Plymouth Court
Architect: Howard Van Doren Shaw

This vigorous design is of generally traditional character, but freely treated so that it seems original rather than imitative. The facade gains interest from the way the arches over some of the openings are played off against the flat heads, or lintels, of others and the greater openness of the upper stories against the greater solidness of the lower two. The spandrels in the upper stories, and the window glass throughout, are set well back from the surfaces of the piers to show their mass, which contributes greatly to the vigor and strength of the whole design. The centerpiece, around the doors, is interesting in its modifications of classical motifs. The coat-of-arms, with its Indian head and the representation of Fort Dearborn in relief, and the medallions refer to series of books published by the Lakeside Press.

42

Pontiac Building (1891)   NR
542 South Dearborn Street
Architects: Holabird & Roche

The Pontiac is the oldest surviving downtown building designed by Holabird & Roche. Its simply treated brick walls and gently projecting oriels are reminiscent of Burnham & Root's Monadnock Building of the same year. In the Pontiac, however, the exterior walls do not support the building but rather form a taut skin that sheathes the skeleton frame. The frame is less forcefully expressed here than in other Holabird & Roche facades. Here, the wide oriels of the east and west facades span two structural bays; consequently, at the center of each of these oriels is a vertical member of the frame that is not expressed on the exterior.

While the expression of the structural frame has come to represent the Chicago school, Holabird & Roche, unburdened by such foreknowledge, seem to have been exploring here the expression of the wall as a thin and flexible basis for form.

43

Dwight Building (1911)
626 South Clark Street
Architects: Schmidt, Garden & Martin

This building shows the application of the general principles of design seen in the Montgomery Ward Warehouse (90) to an office building. Similar framing strips can be seen on the horizontals but here are limited to the upper edge of these members. Hardly interrupting the upward movement of the wall, these accents distinguish the sills from the heads of the windows and emphasize the agreeable horizontal proportions of the windows themselves.

LaSalle Street Canyon

44 Chicago Board of Trade

Federal Reserve Bank Building (1922)
230 South LaSalle Street
Architects: Graham, Anderson, Probst & White

45 Continental Illinois Bank

208 South LaSalle Street Building (1914)
Architects: D. H. Burnham & Company

46 Rookery

190 South LaSalle Street Building (1986)
Architects: John Burgee with Philip Johnson

47 LaSalle National Bank Building

State Bank Building (1928)
Southwest corner of Monroe and LaSalle streets
Architects: Graham, Anderson, Probst & White

Northern Trust Building (1905, 1930)
50 South La Salle Street
Architects: Frost & Granger

New York Life Building (1894, 1898)
Northeast corner of Monroe and LaSalle streets
Architects: Jenney & Mundie

Central YMCA Building (1893)
19 South LaSalle Street
Architects: Jenney & Mundie

Lumber Exchange Building (1913–15)
11 South LaSalle Street
Architects: Holabird & Roche

One North LaSalle Building (1930)
Architects: Vitzthum & Burns

American National Bank (1930)
33 North LaSalle Street
Architects: Graham, Anderson, Probst & White

48 Savings of America Tower

In the heart of the Loop is the LaSalle Street canyon, focusing with great intensity on the base and tower of Holabird & Root's Chicago Board of Trade Building. Unlike ensembles in the central area that derive their effect either from natural elements, such as the lake front for the Michigan Avenue cliff and the river for the Michigan Avenue Bridge group and the riverfront overall, or from zones of interchange, such as the rail terminal on Printers' Row, the LaSalle Street canyon derives its power from the exploitation of a rare event in the city's gridded plan. The grid, particularly in the Loop, is based on a square block. This means that, on its flat site, one can regularly look along any street flanked by very tall buildings and still see, whether over the lake or over the prairie, a great pool of light at the end of the compressed vista.

Since the nineteenth century, the Chicago Board of Trade Building has closed such a vista at the foot of LaSalle Street. Here is the commercial and speculative heart of the city. The Chicago Board of Trade tower faces north and is thus almost always seen in shadow or artificially illuminated, intensifying the character of the street. In addition, LaSalle Street narrows in several steps as it approaches the Chicago Board of Trade and this forces the perspective that also contributes to the power of the canyon. The new, narrow tower at 120 North LaSalle, by Helmut Jahn, is only the most recent building to use this condition to powerful effect.

The quality and variety of shadow along LaSalle Street, where the probity of very large, very conservative law firms blends with the raw speculation of traders in the exchanges, have been represented most recently in the only building in Chicago to bear the hand of the New York office of Cleveland-born Philip Johnson and Chicago native John Burgee. Their 190 South LaSalle building is a shade of another sort, wherein the building's form recalls the long since demolished Masonic

Temple of 1892 by Burnham & Root, while its elevations recall the punched opening masonry walls of modernist buildings of the 1950s.

Just north of the Board of Trade are the facing pediments of the Federal Reserve and Continental Illinois banks. Reflecting an ancient hierarchy, the Federal Reserve uses the Corinthian order for its columns, while the Continental Illinois Bank acknowledges its slightly lower status by using the Ionic order. Both however, defer to the Art Deco form of the Board of Trade, defining as it does, the central private economic power of the city. They also complete the compression and narrowing of the street by having the only porticoes that project from the building mass. The vertical edges of the street's buildings seem in perspective to step down as they approach the tower of the Chicago Board of Trade. The porticoes of the banks participate in a series of horizontal steps, from the plane of the street to the porticoes themselves, to the extremely refined and abstracted planar pediment of the Chicago Board of Trade entrance block, capped as it is by the two carved figures of trade, which create a split acroterion, and terminating, finally, against the sky, in the pyramidal cap of the great center tower.

44

Chicago Board of Trade Building (1930, 1983)
CL, NR

141 West Jackson Boulevard
Architects: Holabird & Root (1930);
   Murphy / Jahn and Shaw, Swanke,
   Hayden & Connell (1983)

The Board of Trade is one of Chicago's best Art Deco skyscrapers, in large part because its massing so perfectly reinforces the perspective view down LaSalle Street and
provides such a forceful termination to the LaSalle Street

canyon. An earlier Board of Trade Building designed by
W. W. Boyington, which occupied the same site from 1885
until 1928, also towered over its neighbors and dramatically
terminated LaSalle Street.

The present structure rests on a nine-story base, which
contained the enormous six-story trading room of the board
(until it was divided horizontally in 1975 to provide additional space needed by the Chicago Board Options Exchange); this space is expressed on the exterior by the tall
windows above the third floor. Above the base a wide tower
rises at the rear of the structure to reach 45 stories. Two
symmetrical projections to the north rise 13 stories above
the base and create a deep setback. This vertical massing is
reinforced by the tall continuous piers of the towers. Horizontal lines are minimized; the spandrels of the towers are
recessed and discontinuous. Atop the pyramidal roof is a
32-foot aluminum statue of Ceres, the Roman goddess of
grain. Designed by sculptor John H. Storrs, it symbolizes
one of the chief commodities traded by the board.

Low entrance corridors flanked by shops lead to a
high three-story lobby that is a masterpiece of Art Deco design. The space is finished in several varieties of contrasting
marble, demonstrating the Art Deco fondness for sleek,
polished surfaces. Translucent glass and nickel reflectors
cast a diffused light that is mirrored in the marble.
Throughout the lobby are examples of the severely rectilinear ornament characteristic of the Art Deco style.

Helmut Jahn's 1983 addition is the first of his series of
buildings which explore the tensions of mimicking masonry
forms with thin curtain walls. Here he has taken the tower
of the original building, made it shorter and fatter for pro-
grammatic purposes, added to the back of the original
building like a bustle, and then capped his new pyramid
with an octagonal element that symbolizes the trading pits
of the exchanges. A more ordinary reading of the form
suggests the hoods and radiator ornaments of the luxury
cars the exchange traders are assumed to drive.

45

Continental Illinois National Bank and Trust Company Building (1924)

231 South LaSalle Street
Architects: Graham, Anderson, Probst & White

Built as the Illinois Merchants Bank, this nineteen-story building expresses both the dignity and grandeur considered appropriate to a banking establishment of the time. With the exception of the tall Ionic columns at the entrance, the facade is simply treated and unadorned. Inside, the enormous banking floor, with its tall columns and high coffered ceiling, is not only a monument to the world of finance but one of the grandest interior spaces in the city. The murals are by Jules Guerin and take as their theme the

peoples of the world set in an environment of buildings derived from the World's Columbian Exposition.

The Continental Bank and the higher-status (expressed through the use of the Corinthian order at the entrance) Federal Reserve Bank across LaSalle Street, also by Graham, Anderson, Probst & White, framed the vista to the 1885 Chicago Board of Trade by W. W. Boyington, a building which had become a pygmy in relation to the giants around it. Graham, Anderson, Probst & White's buildings demonstrated their confidence in the redevelopment of the Board of Trade with a larger and finer building whose scale would be influenced by the context they provided.

46

Rookery Building (1888)   CL, NR
209 South LaSalle Street
Architects: Burnham & Root
Renovations: Frank Lloyd Wright, 1907
    William B. Drummond, ca. 1930

With the Monadnock, the Rookery epitomizes the qualities of the Burnham & Root partnership. Rich and flexible in design, sophisticated and responsive in planning, intelligent and innovative in structure and the use of materials, the whole displays an enormous self-confidence. Not only does the building present a compelling solution, it also suggests alternative possibilities. This is most richly expressed on the ground floor where the power of rusticated wall, the elegance of polished column, and the taut fragility of the windows combine for a seemingly effortless grand effect. Further enhanced by Frank Lloyd Wright's reworking of the atrium and William Drummond's elevator lobbies, the decade-long cleaning and restoration of the building has just been brought to magnificent completion by McClier, following prior work by Hasbrouck-Hunderman, Hasbrouck-Peterson, and Booth/Hansen.

LaSalle National Bank Building   (1934)
(Originally Field Building)
135 South LaSalle Street
Architects: Graham, Anderson, Probst &
   White

This was the last Art Deco skyscraper built in Chicago; indeed, it was the last large office building completed before the twenty-year hiatus in major construction occasioned by the Depression and Second World War. The forms associated with the architecture of the late 1920s have here reached a level of utter purity. Closely ranked vertical bands of windows alternate with narrow, continuous piers to create a verticality that is unrelenting. The long facade of the building extends from LaSalle to Clark, and the shorter facades appear as narrow towers facing the two streets. The central mass is 42 stories high, and is flanked at each corner by a tower half that high. Just as the Art Deco facade pattern has here been purified, so too has the massing characteristic of that style.

A long, two-story lobby connects the LaSalle and Clark Street entrances. Finished in white, beige, and green marble complemented by metal fixtures and mirrored surfaces, it is one of Chicago's best Art Deco lobbies. This light palette of materials is used in this and other buildings of its kind in Chicago with the effervescence of the driest champagne. One half expects to see Fred Astaire dancing across the bridges that span the lobby. At the central bank of elevators is a mail drop and elevator panel in the shape of the building itself.

William LeBaron Jenney's Home Insurance Building occupied this site from 1884 until 1929. During its demolition a committee of Chicago architects examined the building's structure and declared it the first true skyscraper. Subsequent scholars have challenged this claim with plausible arguments but no definitive result.

Savings of America Tower (1992)
120 North LaSalle Street
Architects: Murphy/Jahn

For some time Helmut Jahn has been exploring the relation
between the presence of stone-clad office buildings and the
modernist demands for the expression of the structural
frame enclosed with a curtain wall. Here, on a tight, relatively narrow mid-block site, he has used stone to convey
weight and curtain wall to convey lightness to stunning effect. The building is most notable from the street for its
large mosaic by Roger Brown of two decidedly wingtip
types in the roles of Daedalus and Icarus. For such a slim
rectangular site, Jahn has introduced substantial curves on
every axis—at the top, in the mosaic, and most effectively,
as the device to exploit the progressive narrowing of La-
Salle Street toward the Chicago Board of Trade.

City Hall–County Building (1911)   CL
LaSalle, Randolph, Clark, and Washington
  streets
Architects: Holabird & Roche

This colossal monolithic neoclassical structure covers an entire city block. When viewed from the Daley Center Plaza to the east, it makes a most impressive backdrop to this great downtown open space. Actually, the structure is composed of two buildings linked by passageways at various levels: City Hall is the west half, the County Building the east half. The original design called for a domed center which was never constructed for reasons of cost. The building is 12 stories high, with two basements. The exterior is principally granite. Green terra-cotta, in imitation of patinated bronze, is used in some window bays. The top story is also clad in terra-cotta. The City Council Chamber is on the second floor (LaSalle Street) and the Mayor's office and County Board offices are on the fifth. The spacious lobbies on the first floor with their vaulted ceilings covered with mosaics provide an impressive entry to this monumental civic building.

James R. Thompson Center (1985)
Randolph, LaSalle, Lake, and Clark streets
Architects: Murphy/Jahn

The James R. Thompson Center has been by far the most controversial yet engrossing building erected in the Loop during the past several decades. The issues of the debate surrounding it are not only aesthetic and practical but political as well. Formally, the building's huge, sloping, aggressively curvilinear glass facade mounted by a diagonally truncated glass cylinder, deviates strikingly from the prevailing rectilinearity of Chicago's downtown architecture. To some observers, Helmut Jahn's design is a powerfully original invention, to others, a contextual blasphemy. Functionally, because the exterior is so heavily lined with glass exposed to the sun, the heating and ventilation system has never fully protected the 17-story atrium space against extreme interior temperature fluctuations. Complaints about noise persist from employees who work in the partition-free offices bordering the atrium.

Whether the James R. Thompson Center is a spectacular extravagance reflective of the clamorous ambitions of the governor who promoted it, and for whom it was renamed, or a brilliantly original work made possible by the same man's courageous patronage, the building is an urban cynosure. Its very siting attracts attention, situated as it is across from the Chicago City Hall and the Daley Center, two other buildings of architectural distinction and governmental import. Sight lines from the plaza of the Daley Center make it highly visible. Its great southwest to northeast curve is fronted by a rank of large freestanding granite posts that converge upon an abstract sculpture by Jean Dubuffet (cheerfully dubbed by the public "Snoopy in a Blender") at the northwest corner of Randolph and Clark Streets. The north and west facades are flat and less interesting.

In the interior all but the lower stories are open to the atrium. The banks of elevators and staircases also protrude into that space, producing the vision of a concave surface seen by some as bedazzling, by others as cacophonous. A large circular opening in the street floor leads downward to refectory services at basement level. Color abounds throughout, adding further to one of the most visually arresting architectural phenomena in the city.

51

Brooks Building (1910)
223 West Jackson Boulevard
Architects: Holabird & Roche

A late work of the Chicago school, the Brooks Building has a spectacularly open facade that directly reflects the skeleton frame. A strong vertical emphasis is created by the division of each pier into a cluster of long narrow columns and by the vertical moldings within each horizontal spandrel. The piers terminate in a burst of ornament reminiscent of that at the tops of the piers of the Gage Group (9), which

Louis Sullivan designed in collaboration with Holabird &
Roche in 1898—although here perhaps the ornament is
better integrated with the rest of the facade. Note the variation of the "Chicago window"; here a slightly wider movable sash replaces the typical central stationary pane of
glass.

52

Union Station   (1925)
Canal Street between Adams Street and
    Jackson Boulevard
Architects: Graham, Burnham & Company
    (1913–17); Graham, Anderson, Probst &
    White (after 1917)

The Union Station complex originally consisted of two
separate structures on either side of Canal Street, connected
below grade by a broad vaulted tunnel. The larger structure is the 8-story headhouse that still stands on the west

side of Canal Street. Early plans for the complex incorporated the headhouse into a 20-story office building, and the existing foundations are sufficient to support such a structure. This project was designed and announced in 1990 but has yet to begin. Above its colonnaded base, the headhouse as built has a simple office-block facade. Only the high colonnade and wide entrances at the centers of the north and south facades mark it as a train station. Inside the headhouse, stairs lead down into the main waiting room. This monumental space is 112 feet high to the top of its vaulted skylight, and is surrounded by enormous Corinthian columns that contribute to its grand scale. Two freestanding columns supporting allegorical figures of Day and Night mark the entrance to the below-grade passageway that originally led to the concourse building on the east side of Canal.

The concourse building was a classically styled, pedimented structure that was demolished in 1969 and replaced by an office building. This eastern building contained the vast passenger concourse that was the most impressive space

in the station complex. Modeled on the concourse of New York's Pennsylvania Station (now also demolished), the space was roofed by three parallel glass and tile vaults carried on steel arch ribs which were supported by steel lattice columns. At the north and south sides of the passenger concourse were low train concourses that ended in train platforms and tracks.

The station serves two separate sets of tracks, ten extending to the north and fourteen to the south. It has been estimated that the station can easily accommodate a total of 720 trains and 400,000 passengers a day, although it has rarely handled more than half those numbers.

Union Station is a model of efficient planning for a tremendous volume of traffic. All areas used by the passenger—ticket offices, baggage checks, waiting rooms, concourse, and platforms—are on one level, isolated from the level where baggage, mail, and freight are handled.

St. Patrick Church (1856)   CL, NR
718 West Adams Street
Architects: Carter & Bauer

Chicago's oldest surviving church building, St. Patrick is an example of the Romanesque revival style (often called Norman in the 1850s) characterized by round arches, narrow windows, and broad massive walls. Typical of the style also are the "blind arcades" or arched "corbel-tables" (thickened horizontal strips of wall carried on masonry projections called "corbels"). The small octagonal towers are not ineffective, given the scale of the narrow arched windows. Originally the center of the facade ended in a gable at the top, and there were no belfry stories or spires on the towers (although they doubtless were intended from the beginning).

The Chicago River Front and Wacker Drive

River City (1984)
800 South Wells Street
Architects: Bertrand Goldberg & Associates

311 South Wacker Drive (1991)
Architects: Kohn Pedersen Fox

54 Sears Tower

55 Hartford Plaza Buildings

56 U.S. Gypsum (1963–1994)

One South Wacker (1983)
Architects: Murphy/Jahn

Chicago Mercantile Exchange (1983, 1986)
10 and 30 South Wacker Drive
Architects: Fujikawa, Johnson Associates

57 Civic Opera House

58 Riverside Plaza (Chicago Daily News)

59 Citicorp Center

Rubloff Building (1986)
123 North Wacker Drive
Architects: Perkins & Will

60 Morton International

One Northwestern Center (1913)
11 North Canal Street
Architects: Graham, Burnham & Company

River Center (1922)
111 North Canal Street
Architects: D. H. Burnham & Company

61 333 West Wacker Drive

225 West Wacker Drive (1989)
Architects: Kohn Pedersen Fox and Perkins & Will

Chicago Times Building (1927)
211 West Wacker Drive
Architects: Holabird & Roche

Engineering Building (1928)
205 West Wacker Drive
Architects: Burnham Brothers

62 Merchandise Mart

Builders Building (1927, 1986)
222 North LaSalle Street
Architects: Graham, Anderson, Probst & White;
Skidmore, Owings & Merrill

63 City of Chicago Central Office Building

LaSalle-Wacker Building (1930)
221 North LaSalle Street
Architects: Holabird & Root; Andrew Rebori,
Associate

R. R. Donnelley Building (1992)
Architects: Ricardo Bofill Arquitectura/Taller U.S.A.;
with DeStefano/Goettsch

Ryan Insurance (1968)
55 West Wacker Drive
Architects: C. F. Murphy Associates

Leo Burnett Building (1989)
35 West Wacker Drive
Architects: Kevin Roche–John Dinkeloo & Associates

64 Marina City

65 IBM Building

Sun-Times Building (1957)
401 North Wabash Avenue
Architects: Naess & Murphy

66 Jewelers Building

67 Seventeenth Church of Christ Scientist

Mather Tower (1928)
75 East Wacker Drive
Architect: Herbert H. Riddle

Illinois Center (1967–)
East Wacker Drive east of Michigan Avenue
Architect: Ludwig Mies van der Rohe and successors

Cityfront Center (1985–)
North Bank of Chicago River, east of the Equitable
Building
Architects: Initial Plan, Cooper, Eckstut; Ongoing Plan, Lo-
han Associates; Skidmore, Owings & Merrill

The visual axis of the main branch of the Chicago River when approached from Lake Michigan seems to be starkly terminated by the black east elevation of Mies van der Rohe's IBM Building with a force like that of the slab that keeps popping up in Stanley Kubrick's *2001: A Space Odyssey*. The main and south branches of the river just outside the Loop are the city's psychic main street, where the dreams of Chicagoans flow from deep within the city to join the ambition, desire, and fantasy of the center. Today the river corridor approaches the completion of a vision for the riverfront begun with Burnham's 1909 Plan. The City's numerous bridges and strip parks along the river edge provide a public context for a sequence of buildings of unfolding power and drama, which address both the river and the skyline. Just as Mies's IBM marks the gateway to the river and the city, Kohn Pedersen Fox's 333 West Wacker Drive marks the turn from the main to the south branch of the river. Two elements often claimed to be destructive of urban qualities and values—modern architecture and the American urban grid—have here provided urbane gestures that benefit the city's form enormously. In some cases architects have designed background buildings for the foreground sites of the riverfront, as in the efforts of Bofill and Roche at 77 and 35 West Wacker. On the other hand, the slightly jumpy assertiveness of the Morton International Building provides as rewarding a solution to a difficult site as the more relaxed Daily News Building to its south.

East and West Wacker Drive border the south side of the main branch of the river before turning south, where North and South Wacker Drive have been developed as a wide boulevard of towers one block east of the south branch of the river. The emergence of cars from and their disappearance into Lower Wacker Drive is exciting for its unexpectedness. The buildings on the west side of Wacker Drive enjoy frontage on the river. Many of them exploit this dual quality, often by inserting pedestrian passages along the river's edge.

54

Sears Tower   (1974)
Block bounded by Franklin Street and Wacker
   Drive, Adams Street, and Jackson Boulevard
Architects: Skidmore, Owings & Merrill

The bold stepped-back silhouette of the Sears Tower dominates Chicago's skyline with strength and élan. At 1,454
feet (110 stories), it is the world's tallest building, exceeding
New York's twin-towered World Trade Center by 100 feet
and Chicago's Amoco Building by 330 feet. The structural
steel frame is sheathed in black aluminum and bronze-
tinted glass. The structure consists of nine framed tubes,
each 75 feet square. These tubes are bundled together
structurally to form a mega-tube that provides lateral
strength to withstand wind loads. The nine tubes rise together for 49 stories, where the northwest and southeast
tubes terminate. The building rises as a Z through the next
sixteen stories. At the sixty-fifth floor, the northeast and
southwest tubes stop, and the building continues as a cruciform to the ninetieth floor. There, the remaining north,
east, and south tubes end, creating a rectangular tower that
rises 20 stories to reach the full height. The resulting pattern of setbacks and the flush wall planes recall the skyscrapers of the late 1920s and early 1930s. Sears, Roebuck & Company occupied the very large lower floors, which their work
required, until moving those employees to a suburban facility in 1992.

The original base and confusing entrance to the building, set on a windswept granite plaza, was not redeemed by
Alexander Calder's *Universe,* a spiraling and swinging sculpture located in the lobby. In 1985, Skidmore, Owings &
Merrill added a rural mailbox shaped atrium at the west
entrance. In 1994 DeStefano and Partners redesigned the
entire entry sequence on the east, south and west sides of
the building giving tenants and visitors to the building a
clearer and more dramatic entry experience.

55

Hartford Plaza Buildings (1961, 1971)
100 and 150 South Wacker Drive
Architects: Skidmore, Owings & Merrill

These buildings demonstrate an interesting solution in one
of today's chief areas for experiment: the treatment of the
"wall" of a skyscraper. At 100 South Wacker the glass is
hung back deep within a reinforced concrete frame, providing functional advantages, such as shading the glass area
and giving easier access for washing it. The primary value,
however, is aesthetic—the introduction of an interesting
depth into the facade. The horizontal members of the concrete frame are slightly curved on their undersides, expressing the forces of the building's structure, greatly enlivening
the design. The concrete frame is surfaced in light gray
granite.

The southern building, designed by the same architects for the same owners, offers a striking contrast in color and finish of material and in treatment of the wall surface. The walls are of polished black granite and the windows have been set flush with the wall plane, creating a sleek, smooth surface. The only depth is created by the very slight outward flare of the piers at the base.

56

United States Gypsum Building   (1963)
101 South Wacker Drive
Architects: Perkins & Will Partnership

Demolished 1994

The 19-story, steel-framed tower exhibits the novel feature of being turned at 45 degrees to the street lines—a simple planning device which serves to admit light equally to all four elevations, to provide four little triangular plazas on the site, and to interrupt the solid row of fronts extending to the north and south along the drive. The building is the most richly clad of all Chicago office towers. The continuous columns, lying outside the main wall planes, are sheathed in marble; the spandrels are rough-faced slabs of black slate, and the windows are composed of dark glass with a bluish-gray tint. The ceilings above the open areas around the lobby and around the utility core at the top floor are broken up into planes forming shallow dihedral angles, and the column sheathing ends in sharp-pointed finials standing clear above the roof line. The shapes of these various polyhedra were derived from the crystalline structure of calcium sulfate, the chemical name for gypsum. The contrasts of shape, color, and texture in the building's external covering are disciplined by the geometry of the underlying frame, which thus saves it from ostentatious extravagance.

57

Civic Opera Building (1929)
20 North Wacker Drive
Architects: Graham, Anderson, Probst &
   White

Not since Adler and Sullivan's Auditorium of 1889 (3) had such a project been undertaken on so large a scale: a hall for the performance of grand opera has here been incorporated into a major structure that serves other functions. The Civic Opera House was successor to the Auditorium in another way. After the Opera House opened in 1929, opera and other musical events were regularly booked here rather than at the Auditorium, which led to the eventual closing of the earlier hall.

This building is impressive for its structural achievement as well as for its architectural design. Carrying the weight of a massive office tower above a base that contains the void of two large theaters required a complex system of enormous trusses that transfer loads at various levels. In design, the building is typical of the office buildings of the late 1920s. Above the thirteenth floor of the river facade is a deep setback. The vertical bands of windows and continuous piers are also characteristic of the late 1920s. The Wacker Drive facade is a broad plane unbroken by setbacks. At its base an impressive colonnade covers the sidewalk and terminates at each end in a pedimented entrance to one of the auditoriums.

The Opera lobby is richly developed and the theater is highlighted by Jules Guerin's fire curtain painted with vignettes of grand opera.

58

Riverside Plaza (1929)
400 West Madison Street
Architects: Holabird & Root

Originally the Chicago Daily News Building, this was the first Chicago building to be erected on railroad air rights, in this case on the north track layout of the recently completed Union Station. By placing the narrow office block on the west edge of the site, the architects opened half of the lot area to a broad and generous plaza that faces the Civic Opera on the east side of the river. The simple slablike form of the steel-framed building; the vertical bands suggesting piers or pilasters at the base, end bays, and top; the blocklike masses of the wings; and the emphatic symmetry are all distinguishing features of the purified skyscraper style that flourished briefly in the late 1920s.

The southern wing contains a corridor connecting the riverfront to the Citicorp Center. The mural by John Norton that formerly adorned the corridor ceiling has been re-

moved, with the building management's expressed intention that it will be fully restored.

59

Citicorp Center (1987)
500 West Madison Street
Architects: Murphy/Jahn

Sited among the cluster of high-rise structures that have quickened growth along the west edge of the downtown business district, this building was achieved only at the price of losing one of the great Guastavino-vaulted buildings of the early twentieth century, the old Chicago & North Western station. Most of the 1,600,000 square feet of the new building are allocated to office floors, while the lower reaches contain the new terminal facilities. To re-awaken the sense of the vast interior that so distinguished

the former building, Murphy/Jahn have here created a
lobby 80 feet high, with 80,000 square feet of floor area
bordered by shops and standard terminal accoutrements.
The space is mammoth, made palpably more so by the
powerful play of structural beams and columns that make a
strong first—or last—impression of architectural Chicago
on anyone arriving in or departing from the city.

Morton International Building (1990)

100 North Riverside Plaza
Architects: Perkins & Will

The importance of this building rests on the canny manner
in which the designers have adopted a program mindful of
concerns early modernism tended to gloss over, while
avoiding the historical costuming associated with most post-
modernist styles. The conscious bow to the riverfront made
on the colonnaded and landscaped east side of the building
is the most obvious evidence of an awareness of physical
context, while such lesser but noteworthy ancient devices as
a clocktower and a marble-clad lobby recall skyscrapers of
1910–20. Nonetheless, all of these elements are carried out
in strongly structural rectilinearity reminiscent of Chicago's
traditional commercial architecture. The frame remains
vigorously expressed, although it appears in a variety of
forms. Even a roof truss from which the southern extension
is suspended brings the Miesian example to mind.

333 West Wacker Drive (1983)
Architects: Kohn Pedersen Fox

333 W. Wacker is more than a competent exercise in contextualism. It makes rare architectural drama of the union of its site and its form. Thrusting up from the sharp turn of the Chicago River at the northwest corner of the central business district, its 365-foot-wide curving, green-tinted reflective glass facade is easily and strikingly visible from the rail and auto lines that lead from the North Side into the downtown area. From that standpoint it is an arresting monolithic gatepost signaling the center of the city. At the same time the serrated angles of its streetside, or southeast, elevation are in comparable accord with the denser, tighter environment of the Loop.

This is the first Chicago building by Kohn Pedersen Fox and the only one by that New York firm completed locally in the modernist mode. The firm adopted a post-modernist idiom for its several later commissions downtown. Even so, a hint of post-modern historicism and an intentional ambiguity currently labeled double coding is evident in the neo-Art Deco striped marble that distinguishes the lowest of the 36 stories from the minimalist surfaces of its upper ranges. The differentiation of the base from the office floors above it has a functional rationale as well: it houses the building's mechanical facilities.

Merchandise Mart (1931)

The River (north bank) between Wells and
Orleans streets
Architects: Graham, Anderson, Probst &
White

Built by Marshall Field and Company to replace and expand in function H. H. Richardson's Marshall Field Wholesale Store, this was the largest building in the world in
floor area until the Pentagon was built in Washington, D.C.
It is also notable as one of the sites of the "markets" of furniture and furnishings, attended by buyers from all over
the country, in which new offerings are displayed in show-
rooms maintained by manufacturers. The style is the Moderne of the 1920s.

Graham, Anderson, Probst & White conducted the
cleaning and renovation of the building from 1986–91. Be-
yer, Blinder, Belle of New York converted the first and second floors into an interior shopping arcade.

City of Chicago Central Office Building (1913)

CL, NR

(Originally Reid, Murdoch and Company)
320 North Clark Street
Architect: George C. Nimmons

This structure is typical of a number of buildings designed by Nimmons for commercial or manufacturing use. It is simple and straightforward, although with some traditional feeling, as in the massiveness emphasized at points here. The brick is used very effectively for its texture and pattern, finely set off by terra-cotta accents. The building is now well maintained and gives a good idea of the original, although it has been remodeled, one bay having been removed from its west side when LaSalle Street was widened. It is one of the first buildings to face the river in accordance with the Burnham Plan of 1909.

Marina City (1964, 1967)
The River (north bank) between State and
  Dearborn streets
Architects: Bertrand Goldberg Associates

Affectionately called the corn cobs, this tightly unified complex embraces apartments, garages, restaurants, office building, bank, marina, television studio, and theater. The two
60-story apartment towers are of concrete construction in
which the loads are carried mainly by cylindrical cores.
The parking space is a helical slab rising continuously
through the first 18 stories of each tower. The pie-shaped
rooms extend into rings of semicircular balconies, which
transform the smooth cylinders into lively repetitive patterns.

IBM Building (1971)
The River (north bank) between Wabash
  and State Streets
Architects: Office of Mies van der Rohe and
  C. F. Murphy Associates

This is the last and the tallest office building designed by
Ludwig Mies van der Rohe, and a bust of the architect by
Marino Marini is in the high-ceilinged, travertine and glass
lobby.

The superbly proportioned tower with its precisely detailed curtain wall achieves the elegant simplicity characteristic of the architect's work during the last decades of his
life. The refined simplicity belies the complex problems of
this particular site. For its regional office building in Chicago, IBM acquired a K-shaped riverfront site bisected at
grade level by a railroad spur. Initially, a U-shaped structure was planned, but the city agreed to eliminate part of
Wabash Avenue so that the site would better accommodate
a rectangular structure. On-site parking requirements were
modified because the rail tracks beneath the structure made
it impossible to provide the required spaces. However, a
parking garage sheathed in Cor-ten steel was designed by
George Schipporeit and built just to the north in 1972.

The tower is 52 stories high and has a curtain wall of
dark aluminum and bronze-tinted glass. The bays of the
structural steel skeleton are 30 feet wide and 40 feet long.
The mechanical systems of the building are extremely sophisticated, in large part because of the controlled environment necessary for areas housing computers. Temperatures
are controlled by a computer, and the heat given off by
lights, machines, and people inside the building is re-
claimed by a reverse refrigeration cycle. Heat transfer between exterior and interior is reduced by a plastic thermal
barrier that separates the curtain wall from the frame. Ex-
ploiting this technical device, the building is fully illuminated at night by the interior lights, creating the
appearance of a pillar of light.

The building occupies a prominent riverfront site. Its
plaza is part of the continuous ground plane of the building, and it terminates high above the river, without providing access to a lower level as some other buildings along the
river do.

35 East Wacker Drive (1926)
(Originally Jewelers Building)
Architects: Giaver & Dinkelberg in association with
Thielbar & Fugard

This lavishly ornamented office structure was built for jew-
elry concerns, hence its original name (the letters "JB" are
worked into the ornament extensively). The cream-colored
terra-cotta that covers the building has been molded into
neobaroque ornament. Atop each corner of the 24-story
main block is a round, domed pavilion on columns. The

17-story tower is crowned with a larger enclosed pavilion.
Originally a parking garage occupied the central portion of
each of the first 22 floors. A tenant could drive into the
building from the lower level of Wacker Drive and enter an
elevator, whereupon the car, but not the driver, would be
lifted to the appropriate floor. This unique arrangement
was abandoned after fourteen years for various reasons.
The space occupied by the elevator shafts was then converted to office use.

67

Seventeenth Church of Christ, Scientist (1968)
Heald Square, East Wacker Drive at
  Wabash Avenue
Architects: Harry Weese & Associates

A powerful semicylindrical form enables this low church
building to hold its own on a visually prominent site
surrounded by taller structures. This assertive form also
expresses the major interior space: a large, rounded auditorium where religious services are conducted. The auditorium rests on reinforced concrete columns and girders
clearly visible at ground level. A bronze-and-glass lobby is
recessed behind a sunken plaza. The plaza serves not only
to isolate the lobby from traffic and passersby, but also to
admit natural light to the Sunday School rooms below
grade level. Most of the structure is reinforced concrete
sheathed in travertine. Steel girders encased in travertine
support the lead-coated cooper roof and are a major element of the design. Long, slot-like windows at the base of
the conical roof admit natural light to the auditorium, as do
the windows at the base of the drum that crowns the roof.
To the east is a 7-story triangular wing that contains church
offices and meeting rooms, restrooms and lounges, and elevators and mechanical areas.

Michigan Avenue Bridge Group

Michigan Avenue Bridge (1918–20)
Michigan Avenue and the Chicago River
Architect: Edward H. Bennett
Engineer: Hugh Young
Sculptors: North end, James E. Fraser; South end,
Henry Hering

68 Wrigley Building

69 Tribune Tower

70 Equitable Building

71 333 North Michigan Avenue

72 360 North Michigan Avenue

Crossing the three branches of the Chicago River has
been the subject of intense concern throughout the city's
history. With the development of the double-leaf trun-
nion bascule bridge, all but one of the bridges built over
the city's waterways since 1903 have been of this type. It
combines advantages for both land and water traffic in
its quickness and ease of operation. The most impressive
of all these bridges is at the intersection of Michigan
Avenue and the main branch of the river. Built between
1918 and 1920, it linked Michigan Avenue facing Grant
Park to the commercially growing extension of the avenue north to Oak Street and Lake Michigan. A collaboration of the architect Edward H. Bennett and the
engineer Hugh Young, the double decked bridge allows
traffic to serve both the upper and lower levels of the
avenue and provides efficient service access on the lower
level to Wacker Drive, which parallels the river.

When the bridge was sited, the angle of the roads it connected created opportunities for axial exploitation at its northwest and southeast corners, and visual drama at the other two corners. Four of the five buildings that frame this great urban space—most of which is given over to the roadway of the bridge and the river below— were built within the decade following the completion of the bridge. However, while three use Bedford limestone and one is sheathed in white glazed terra-cotta, each creates or recalls a different architectural source. Once again, these buildings share a general massing— blocks surmounted by distinct towers—and an idea of the nature of the ensemble in which each has a role to play, in which none is subservient. At night the brilliant illumination of the Wrigley Building serves to relate Michigan Avenue facing Grant Park with the extension of Michigan Avenue north of the bridge.

68

Wrigley Building (1921, 1924)
410 North Michigan Avenue
Architects: Graham, Anderson, Probst &
    White

The Wrigley Building is the earliest of the celebrated skyscraper group at Michigan and the Chicago River. It was floodlit from the beginning and, because of the almost white terra-cotta sheathing, furnished visitors of the 1920s with a dazzling sight. The tower was modeled on the Giralda of the cathedral in Seville. Behind the thin screen that unites the main building and its annex is a handsome little plaza with plantings and a fountain nicely scaled to the narrow area. Louis Solomon and John Cordwell designed the plaza in 1957; Powell/Kleinschmidt restored the lobby in 1984.

The building's facade has never been restored. Instead it has received a continuous program of maintenance, including cleaning, pointing, repair, and when necessary the replacement of the terra-cotta.

69

Tribune Tower (1923–25) CL
435 North Michigan Avenue
Architects: John Mead Howells, Raymond
  M. Hood, Associated Architects

Tribune Tower is familiar to the general public as the home
of the *Chicago Tribune* and among architects and students
of architecture as the winning design in an international
competition held by the *Tribune* in 1922. Although this
Gothic revival design won first place, the wide discussion of

the award led to general agreement that the modern office building, or skyscraper, should be designed in a modern style. The virtues of this building include an active and picturesque silhouette and the interesting treatment of the wall, with vertical sections of different widths. It is modelled on the Butter Tower of Rouen Cathedral. The facade is also inset with stones from famous buildings throughout the world. The Office of John Vinci restored the building in 1991.

The simpler structure joined to the tower on the east was built as a separate building, the Tribune Plant, designed by architect Jarvis Hunt. Its south side was surfaced with stone in 1965.

70

Equitable Building (1965)
401 North Michigan Avenue
Architects: Skidmore, Owings & Merrill;
   Alfred Shaw, Associated

The Equitable Building is noteworthy for the collaboration of owners and architects in reserving a large area as a plaza for a downtown commercial building, thus achieving an openness all too often lacking in skyscrapers that are built to the legal limit of the lot area.

The design is interesting in the way it explores the possibilities of the four-window scheme—the outer two windows narrower than the inner ones—which was used with such subtlety in the 860–880 Lake Shore Drive Apartments (79). Here the difference in width is more obvious, and the effect thus perhaps more dramatic. A pleasant tension arises in each group of four windows from the contrast of the central pair, which are nearly square, with the outer pair, which are clearly vertical rectangles. The horizontal strip of greenish-black marble below the windows adds very different horizontal rectangles which echo the horizontals of the floors. This interesting tension, or play of shapes, helps give the building a "presence" often lacking in contemporary buildings and aided here by the warm tonality coming from the beige color of the aluminum sheathing and the light bronze-tinted glass. The projecting verticals of the exterior not only set the larger units of the design but are also used in practical ways. For instance, the "piers" between the groups of four windows, although not structural—being merely shells set outside the structural piers—carry inside them cylindrical conduits through which hot or cold air is pumped to the offices from floors housing machinery at the top and bottom of the building.

71

333 North Michigan Avenue (1928)
Architects: Holabird & Root

Based on Eliel Saarinen's influential—but only second-prize-winning—entry in the 1922 competition for the design of Tribune Tower, this was one of the distinctive skyscrapers built in Chicago during the late 1920s and early 1930s. These buildings are marked by their forceful verti-

cality—achieved through successive setbacks, strongly articulated vertical piers, and long, vertical bands of windows.
Building planes are flat, and smoothly finished materials
are used extensively. Ornament is in very low relief and
consists of highly stylized, severely geometric forms. Cornices are never used. The Art Deco style freed the skyscraper from the historical forms that had dominated it
since the Columbian Exposition of 1893. The major practitioners of this style in Chicago were Graham, Anderson,
Probst & White and Holabird & Root.

This long, narrow, slablike building rises 24 stories
and has a tower that rises to 35 stories at the northern end.
Above a 4-story, polished marble base, the structure is clad
in limestone. Framing the windows of the fifth floor is incised ornament portraying scenes from early Chicago history. Vertical bands of windows appear on the three sides of
the northern tower.

The building is superbly sited. By orienting the facade
toward the north, the architects provided a handsome termination to the vista down Michigan Avenue from Oak
Street.

72

360 North Michigan Avenue (1923)
(Originally London Guarantee Building)
360 North Michigan Avenue
Architect: Alfred S. Alschuler

Because of its irregular site where Wacker Drive curves to
meet Michigan Avenue, this 21-story building has a vaguely
trapezoidal plan. The east facade follows the regular north-
south line of Michigan Avenue and is broken above the
fifth floor by a deep light court. The west facade angles
away to follow Wacker Drive, and the north side is broken
to create a concave facade oriented toward the river. The 5-
story base and 3-story top display ornamental forms derived
from classical precedents, while the central floors exhibit

the vertical bands of windows and strong, continuous piers common to skyscrapers of the late 1920s. Four Corinthian columns flank a central arched entrance and support a classical entablature, forming a grand entrance that dominates the base. A classical colonnade marks the top stories, the cornice of which is topped by a balustrade. The entire composition is crowned by an elaborate, round, domed pavilion. Less precisely derivative than the towers of the Wrigley or Tribune buildings, this element is related in part to the Choragic Monument of Lysicrates in Athens, although its Corinthian order is much closer to that used on the Tholos at Epidaurus. For his part, Alschuler related the building's termination to the tower of Ragnar Ostberg's then recent Stockholm City Hall.

North Michigan Avenue

Hotel Intercontinental (1927–29)
(originally Medinah Athletic Club)
505 North Michigan Avenue
Architect: Walter W. Ahlschlager

McGraw-Hill Building (1928–29)
520 North Michigan Avenue
Architects: Thielbar & Fugard

Lake Shore Trust and Savings Bank (1921–22)
601 North Michigan Avenue
Architects: Marshall & Fox

Erskine-Danforth Building (1928)
620 North Michigan Avenue
Architect: Philip B. Maher

Women's Chicago Athletic Club (1926–28)
626 North Michigan Avenue
Architect: Philip B. Maher

Crate and Barrel Store (1990)
646 North Michigan Avenue
Architects: Solomon, Cordwell & Buenz

Terra Museum of American Art (1987)
660 North Michigan Avenue
Architects: Booth, Hansen & Associates

Farwell Building (1926–27)
664 North Michigan Avenue
Architect: Philip B. Maher

City Place (1990)
Michigan Avenue at Huron Street
Architects: Loebl, Schlossman & Hackl

Chicago Place (1990)
700 North Michigan Avenue
Architects: Skidmore, Owings & Merrill (retail);
Solomon, Cordwell & Buenz (apartments)

Allerton Hotel (1923–24)
701 North Michigan Avenue
Architects: Murgatroyd & Ogden

Banana Republic Store (1992)
744 North Michigan Avenue
Architects: Robert A. M. Stern & Associates

Olympia Center (1989)
161 East Superior Street, Michigan Avenue at
Superior St. (Neiman-Marcus store)
Architects: Skidmore, Owings & Merrill

73 Old Water Tower and Pumping Station

74 Water Tower Place

75 Fourth Presbyterian Church and Parish House

76 John Hancock Center

900 North Michigan Avenue (1989)
Architects: Kohn Pedersen Fox

77 919 North Michigan Avenue

78 Drake Hotel

One Magnificent Mile (1983)
940–80 North Michigan Avenue
Architects: Skidmore, Owings & Merrill

During the last sixty years, several planned changes in
the character and appearance of North Michigan Avenue
have turned that thoroughfare from a sedate residential
strip into one of the world's great public concourses.

Prior to World War I, when it was known as Pine
Street, it was lined with upscale family homes, and most
of the traffic that passed from it into the Loop was
obliged to cross the river at Rush Street, a block to the
west. Following the recommendations of the Burnham
Plan to create boulevards to alleviate the growing tangle
of traffic throughout the inner area, the city elected to
widen Michigan Avenue north of Randolph Street, to
build a two-level bascule bridge that would connect
Michigan Avenue and Pine Street—with a slight jog in
the route—and to call the whole passage Michigan Ave-

nue. The inevitable consequence was the transformation of North Michigan Avenue into an increasingly commercial district. The Drake Hotel at its north end and the Wrigley Building at the south, both completed within months of each other in 1920–21, were the first buildings to suggest a new identity to the now substantially broadened boulevard. Other large structures followed: the Tribune Tower across from the Wrigley Building, in 1925, and the Allerton Hotel at the corner of Huron, in the previous year. By the beginning of the 1930s, the Moderne manner had made its first appearance on the avenue, in the Medinah Athletic Club just north of Tribune Tower and the Michigan Square Building at Ohio Street. This last structure, by Holabird & Root, was distinguished by the exquisite foyer known as Diana Court, perhaps the finest piece of Art Deco architecture ever realized in Chicago.

The Michigan Square Building, demolished in the early 1970s, was one of the major victims along the avenue of an impulse to tear down that is as historically strong in the Chicago heart as the drive to build. (The amiably eccentric Italian Court at Ontario Street, by Robert de Golyer, and the solid old 900 North Michigan Building, by Jarvis Hunt, are but two of the other prime area casualties.) Both tendencies were reactivated shortly after World War II, when the developer Arthur Rubloff proposed turning North Michigan Avenue, already the city's premier street of shops and restaurants, into what he himself envisioned rather grandly as the "Magnificent Mile."

A plan commissioned in 1947 by Rubloff and designed by Holabird & Root would have included, on each side of the avenue, a row of low-rise buildings with another row behind it, separated by a narrow mall of green. This concept was never realized as intended, but the dream of an ambitiously upgraded Michigan Avenue did materialize in the 1960s, 1970s, and 1980s, largely in response to the socioeconomic decline of the old central business district.

Until the 1950s the Loop had been the multichambered heart of Chicago, its veriest Downtown, where business was transacted by day and entertainment enjoyed by night. But the coincidence of the exurban flight of the white middle class with the wave of immigration of nonwhite ethnic groups into the city made the Loop either unattractive or inaccessible to the people who could best afford to keep it alive. To avoid an economic disaster, that is, to retain or to gain back the white middle class as workers, shoppers, and recreation seekers in the inner city, Chicago's big merchants undertook to turn North Michigan into a second central business district. Water Tower Place, a mammoth urban shopping mall, was the cornerstone of this new enterprise. Often likened in habitual Chicago hyperbole to Paris's Champs Elysées, the avenue of the seventies and eighties came to be known among local wags as the Caucasian Fields.

Notwithstanding the extent to which North Michigan today amounts to an unofficially segregated neighborhood, it is unassailably an impressive architectural phenomenon, not only as a collection of individual buildings but as a discernibly coherent environment. On account of the jog at the bridge at its south end and the vista of the lake immediately beyond its north end, it is an easily perceptible entity, the more pronounced if one studies it from the crest of the gentle slope that carries it northward from the bridge. The old Water Tower at Chicago Avenue only adds a fitting moment of spatial punctuation, a visual shifting of gears, to one of the liveliest and most compelling urban passages in America.

73

Old Chicago Water Tower (1869)   CL, NR
North Michigan Avenue at Chicago Avenue
Architect: W. W. Boyington

Built to house a 138-foot standpipe that was required to
equalize the pressure of the water pumped from the Pumping Station to the east, the Old Chicago Water Tower was
designed by one of Chicago's earliest architects. Boyington's
imitation of Gothic architecture is so naive that it seems

charmingly original at points, as in the cut-stone "battle-ments" at the top of the lower wall sections. Oscar Wilde, on his visit to Chicago in 1882, called it a "castellated monstrosity with pepper boxes stuck all over it," although he praised the pumping machinery as "simple, grand and natural." As one of the few buildings that survived in the path of the Chicago Fire of 1871, the Old Water Tower has become one of the city's most beloved symbols. With the recent development of North Michigan Avenue into a major shopping district, the tower's prominent location has only increased its attractiveness to local citizens and tourists alike.

74

Water Tower Place (1976)
Michigan Avenue, and Chestnut, Seneca,
    and Pearson streets
Architects: Loebl, Schlossman, Dart &
    Hackl; associate architects: C. F. Murphy
    & Associates

Although the exterior resembles a huge marble monolith, colorless and fortresslike, the interior, by Warren Platner, is dazzling with its marble, glass, and chrome appointments and even a waterfall. The ride up the escalator or, better still, the glass-enclosed elevator can be a spectacular experience.

The 12-story base contains a vertical shopping mall and offices. At the southeast section is a 62-story tower containing a Ritz-Carlton Hotel and luxury condominium apartments.

The mall with seven floors is constructed around a great atrium and five courts. More than 100 stores, shops, theaters, and boutiques are contained within about 610,000 square feet of floor space. The eighth and ninth floors contain about 200,000 square feet of office space. On the tenth and eleventh floors are the hotel's health spa facilities and mechanical system, while the twelfth floor is devoted to the hotel lobby and restaurants.

75

**Fourth Presbyterian Church and Parish
House** (1912, 1925)   NR
125 East Chestnut Street
Architects: Ralph Adams Cram; Howard
    Van Doren Shaw

Ralph Adams Cram was one of the leaders of the Gothic
revival in the United States, and his Fourth Presbyterian
Church demonstrates an accurate knowledge of the Gothic
style that contrasts with such naive imitations as Holy Family Church (116) and the Old Chicago Water Tower (73).
However, the Gothic features are here freely modified, as
in the narrowness of the side aisles, the shape of the piers,

and the use of the transept space for a balcony. The severity
of the exterior contrasts with the warmer and more varied
wall surfaces of the adjacent parish house (1925) by Howard Van Doren Shaw. The church is separated from the
parish house by a cloistered walk and serene courtyard that
seem miles away, although actually only a few feet, from
busy North Michigan Avenue.

TO

John Hancock Center   (1969)
North Michigan Avenue between Chestnut
   and Delaware streets
Architects: Skidmore, Owings & Merrill

By far the finest and most interesting of Chicago's giant
buildings, the assertive, muscular John Hancock Center
claims our attention as powerfully as the tapering masonry
Monadnock.

The John Hancock's profile is more graceful and soaring than the rectangular Sears Tower and Amoco Building,
and paradoxically it also gives the impression of maximum
stability. The diagonals add visual interest to the pattern of
columns and girders by establishing a separate but harmonious geometry that serves to lead the eye from the human
scale of the individual windows to the vast technological
scale of the whole structure.

Like Marina City, this is a multifunction building:
there are shops and businesses on the concourse level and
lower floors; 29 stories of office space and 48 stories of
apartments; and an observatory, a two-level restaurant, and
radio and television facilities at the top. The tapering form
of the 1,105-foot structure, in which all four walls are inclined inward from the vertical, was adopted to provide
maximum floor space for public shopping at the base, less
extensive but still substantial areas at the office levels, and
the smallest spaces for the apartments—meanwhile insuring an outside exposure for all rooms.

Like the Sears and Amoco towers, which redesigned their entrances to become user friendly, the Hancock hired Hiltscher Shapiro to reorganize its multilevel entrance and elevator systems. To be completed in 1995, the rectangular sunken plaza will become elliptical in form, water elements will be added, and the signing of the retail shops will be emphasized.

77

919 North Michigan Avenue (1930)
(Previously the Playboy Building, originally
    the Palmolive Building)
919 North Michigan Avenue
Architects: Holabird & Root

This is the northernmost of the Chicago skyscrapers designed in the purified Vertical style of the late 1920s and
early 1930s later known as Art Moderne or Art Deco.
When the building was constructed, the area around it was
developed with much lower structures, and for many years
its wide facade dominated the vista up Michigan Avenue
from the river. Its many symmetrical setbacks create a lively
pattern of receding masses. Ranks of windows set into recessed channels emphasize the strong verticality. Atop the
building is a 150-foot airplane beacon originally named for
Charles A. Lindbergh. It no longer functions as a guide for

airplanes, since taller neighboring buildings have made it obsolete for navigation purposes, and nearby apartment dwellers are not charmed by the brilliance of its light.

The ground-floor shops and elevator lobby were restored in 1982 by Skidmore, Owings & Merrill.

78

Drake Hotel (1920)   NR
Lake Shore Drive, Michigan Avenue, and
    Walton Street
Architects: Marshall & Fox

Among Chicago's most distinguished hostelries, the Drake occupies one of the finest locations in the city, facing Lake Michigan and the Oak Street Beach on the north, Michigan Avenue on the west, and Walton Street, where its main entrance is located, to the south. The architects enjoyed an ample budget in planning this 13-story limestone structure. The lobby and public rooms were conceived in the grand manner, with generous spaces for dining, strolling, shopping, and resting. The guest rooms and corridors are equally unconstrained in size, with large windows that permit excellent views, especially over Lake Michigan.

79

860–880 Lake Shore Drive
Apartments (1952)   NR
860–880 North Lake Shore Drive
Architects: Mies van der Rohe; Pace
   Associates; Holsman, Holsman, Klekamp
   & Taylor

As much as any other buildings anywhere, these two towers provided a model for the vitreous, rectangularly prismatic high-rise structures that dominated the international
architectural landscape of the 1950s and 1960s. Widely admired for their openness and the frank expression of the
frame, 860 and 880 are no less notable for the subtly refined

proportioning of their parts. I-beams attached to the mullions and the main supports effectively counterpose a vertical thrust against the horizontality of the spandrels while providing a three-dimensional qualification to the otherwise flat surfaces. Less important, they help to stiffen the frame.

The siting of the buildings is equally compelling. Each is conceived on a 3-by-5-bay plan, with the north tower revealing its longer side to Lake Shore Drive, the south tower its shorter side. They are situated slightly ajog of each other, with a small area of greenery set in the nook thus created. The effect of this arrangement is to maintain yet punctuate the long cliff of apartment buildings that line this section of Chicago's Gold Coast.

80

Prentice Women's Hospital and Maternity Center and the Northwestern Institute of Psychiatry (1975)
333 East Superior Street
Architects: Bertrand Goldberg Associates

This dramatic and technically innovative building serves Northwestern University as both a women's hospital and a psychiatric hospital. The structure consists of a 4-story rectilinear base and a 7-story quatrefoil tower. The base is of simple column-and-beam construction clad in a curtain wall of metal panels and glass. It houses admissions, administrative, and doctors' offices; labor, delivery, and operating rooms; outpatient psychiatric units; and a cafeteria. The tower springs from and is supported by the central core (which contains elevator shafts and stairwells), making this the first structure of its size in which floors and curtain walls are fully cantilevered from a central core. Such a structural system provides column-free spaces in the tower, where the patients' rooms are located. In plan, the tower consists of two intersecting ovals containing four clusters of rooms radiating out from a central service area. Patients can thus be grouped according to care requirements, while the nursing station is located equidistant from every patient's room, making care most efficient.

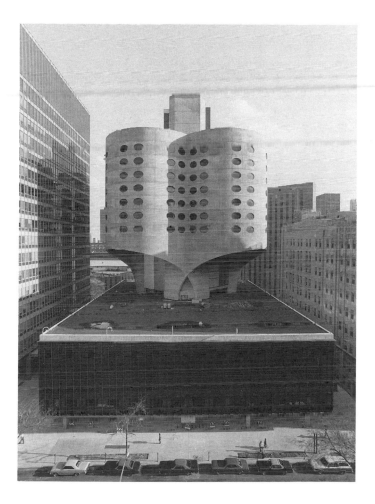

81

Time-Life Building (1970)
541 North Fairbanks Court
Architects: Harry Weese & Associates

This well-proportioned structure is built in reinforced concrete with a curtain wall of gold-tinted reflecting glass
framed by weathering Cor-ten steel that has now turned a
rich, rusty brown. Structural bays are 30 feet square. An
87-foot high base contains a 27-foot-high granite lobby and
several service floors. The lobby is divided into two levels to
accommodate tandem elevators, which were used here for
the first time in the United States. A two-story cab carries
people in the upper portion to even-numbered floors and
those in the lower portion to odd-numbered floors. This
plan reduces elevator shafts 30 percent without decreasing
service.

82

Lake Point Tower (1968)
East Grand Avenue, east of North Lake
   Shore Drive
Architects: Schipporeit-Heinrich Associates;
   Graham, Anderson, Probst & White

The lofty tower that rises close to the western base of Navy
Pier is a celebration of structure; its 645-foot height made it
the highest reinforced concrete building in the world at the
time of its completion, while its flat-slab frame with shear-
wall core in the shape of a triangular prism constitutes a
unique structural system in kind and scale. The three-lobed
shape of the tower was derived from a famous skyscraper
project that Mies van der Rohe proposed for Berlin in 1922.
The young architects who created the design were students
of Mies at Illinois Institute of Technology and later mem-

bers of his office staff. Relative to the conventional rectangular prism, the curved form of Lake Point Tower allowed greater freedom in apartment planning and offered less surface area exposed to direct wind loads. The curtain walls of bronze-tinted glass set in a framework of bronze-anodized aluminum produce reflection patterns of vertical ribbons, ranging in color from intense golden sunlight to deep bronze-black shadows. The two-story base structure extending westward from the tower contains public spaces. It is crowned by a landscaped park designed by Alfred Caldwell with a lagoon and a swimming pool.

83

Navy Pier (1916)
Grand Avenue and Streeter Drive
Architects: Charles Sumner Frost, with
    chief engineer Edward C. Shankland and
    harbor engineer William Artingstall
    (1916); renovations by Jerome R. Butler,
    Jr. (1976); Benjamin Thompson &
    Associates and Vickrey/Ovresat/Awsumb
    (1992–).

Daniel Burnham's Chicago Plan of 1909 called for two large piers extending well into Lake Michigan, each providing for docking and recreational facilities. Only one of them, the 3000 foot long Navy Pier, was constructed. It fulfilled its original purposes more than adequately until the 1930s, when shipping traffic on the Great Lakes dwindled. Thereafter it served as a naval training center during World War II and, from 1946 to 1965, as the home of the Chicago branch of the University of Illinois. Following a decade in which the old structure lapsed into disuse, the city began a long-term reconstruction program. In 1976 the great domed ballroom at the eastern end was restored and by the summer of 1995 the entire pier had been made over into an assortment of indoor and outdoor spaces serving recreation, entertainment, dining, and special events. The most notable features now include the Family Pavilion, with its indoor park and children's museum; the Navy Pier Park, an open area filled with sundry amusements—a ferris wheel, a carousel, a skating rink—as well as a 1500-seat performance tent; and Festival Hall, a 170,000-square-foot facility meant to accommodate expositions and conferences.

The architects are Benjamin Thompson & Associates of Boston and Vickrey/Ovresat/Awsumb Associates of Chicago.

84

Newberry Library (1892, 1983)
60 West Walton Street
Architects: Henry Ives Cobb (1892), Harry
   Weese & Associates (1983)

Containing one of the nation's foremost research collections, the Newberry was built to the specifications of a strong-minded librarian who insisted on such features as hallways constructed almost as separate buildings, in order to preserve quiet in the reading rooms. The robust Romanesque style follows H. H. Richardson's example and was used by Cobb in several other buildings in the Chicago area, such as

the former home of the Chicago Historical Society (88) and the Henry C. Durand Art Institute on the campus of Lake Forest College.

In 1983 Harry Weese & Associates carried out a major program of restoration and refurbishing to much of the interior and attached a massive, brick-clad addition to the northwest corner of the building. The new structure, ten stories high (two of them underground), has added more than 80,000 square feet of stack and storage space to the library. The exterior is marked by incised reliefs of round arches on the north and west elevations and by a pair of cylindrical towers at the corners, one housing a staircase, the other mechanical risers.

85

Quigley Seminary (1918)
Chestnut and Rush streets
Architects: Gustav Steinbeck; Zachary
    Taylor Davis

This neo-Gothic preparatory seminary was established in 1905 by Archbishop James E. Quigley, and construction was carried out after his death by George Cardinal Mundelein. A memorial statue of Archbishop Quigley stands at the corner of Rush and Chestnut.

The French Gothic style that inspired Steinbeck, a New York architect, is evident in the rose window over the chapel entrance, the sculpture on either side, the high pitched roofs, the buttresses on Chestnut Street, and the medieval courtyard. The goal of the designer and client was to reproduce a medieval setting for learning.

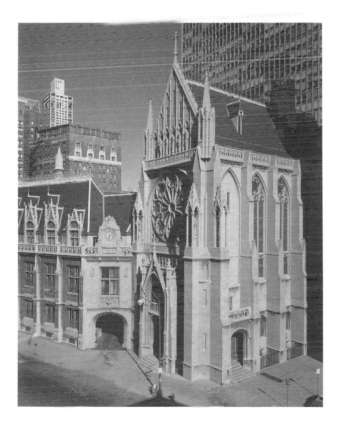

Holy Name Cathedral   (1874)
NE corner of State and Superior streets
Architect: Patrick Charles Keeley;
   remodeled by Henry J. Schlacks (1915);
   renovation by C. F. Murphy & Associates
   (1969)

Holy Name has served as the cathedral of the Roman Catholic Archdiocese of Chicago since 1874. The parish itself began in 1846, at which time it worshiped in the Chapel of the Holy Name on the first floor of the University of St. Mary of the Lake, which then occupied this site. The present church replaced an earlier Gothic edifice built in 1854 and destroyed by the Chicago Fire of 1871. The major material of the building is limestone and the design, simple Late Victorian Gothic. A major renovation was undertaken in 1969; at the time the original foundation was replaced by one of reinforced concrete.

Wabash-Huron-Rush-Erie Block
Cathedral of St. James (1857, 1875)
SE Corner of Wabash Avenue & Huron
    Street
Architects: Burling & Bacchus, Tower (1857)
Edward J. Burling (1875);
Hammond & Roesch, Parish House (1968)

Nickerson Residence (1883)   NR
40 East Erie Street
Architect: Edward J. Burling

John B. Murphy Memorial (1926)
50 East Erie Street
Architects: Marshall & Fox

In the late nineteenth and early twentieth centuries the
neighborhoods along Cass Street (now Wabash Avenue)
and Pine Street (now Michigan Avenue) north of the Chicago River were among the favored preserves of the city's
elite. Three notable architectural works from that period
still stand on the block bounded by Wabash, Huron, Rush,
and Erie.

The parish of St. James, organized in 1834, is the earliest Episcopal parish in Chicago and one of the oldest in Illinois. St. James Church, at Wabash and Huron, became the
cathedral of the Episcopal Diocese of Chicago in 1955. Part
of the present structure, chiefly the tower, dates from the
1857 design, which Burling & Bacchus conceived in the English Gothic tradition, with a handsome wood-beamed
vault commanding the nave. Severely damaged in the Chicago Fire of 1871, the church was rebuilt in 1874–75, in a
form reportedly faithful to the original. Among the numerous changes made over the ensuing decades, the most important has been the redecoration of the interior by the
English-born New York architect E. J. Neville Stent, who
illuminated the nave, transept, and apse with a myriad of
stencils in the Arts and Crafts manner in 1888–89. Stent's

decor was later replaced by other schemes, including that of Thomas Tallmadge in 1925, but the recovery of remaining elements of it furnished the principal inspiration for the brilliant restoration of the church by Holabird & Root in 1985. The space is now one of the most coloristically opulent passages of Chicago's ecclesiastical architecture.

The small Chapel of St. Andrew, located one level below the main sanctuary of the church, was completed in 1913 by Cram, Goodhue & Ferguson after designs by Bertram Goodhue of Boston. It is said to be based on a small abbey chapel in the south of Scotland. To the east is the Parish House by Hammond & Roesch of Chicago, a modernist structure built in 1968 with a clearly articulated and carefully detailed curtain wall. The building is set back from Huron Street, behind a small plaza to the rear of the cathedral.

Adjacent to St. James to the south is the Nickerson Residence, one of the stateliest and best-preserved relics of

Chicago's Gilded Age. The architect, Edward Burling, of Burling & Whitehouse, who also designed St. James, was much sought after by Chicago society of his day. The mansion, built in 1883 of brick about two feet thick and faced with sandstone on three sides, reflects the style of the Italian High Renaissance. The interior, on the other hand, designed by A. Fiedler of New York, is a lavish display of stone and wood more nearly baroque in character. A special gallery meant to accommodate the distinguished Nickerson art collection was also a major feature of the original interior. It was remodeled in 1900 for a later owner, Lucius Fisher, by the Chicago architect George W. Maher.

Since 1919 the Nickerson Residence has been owned by the American College of Surgeons, which uses part of it as administrative offices. The ACS also maintains the impressive auditorium building directly to the east, at 50 East Erie, owned by the John B. Murphy Memorial Association and built in honor of Murphy, a renowned Chicago surgeon. Completed in 1926 after designs by Marshall & Fox of Chicago, the structure bears a striking resemblance to the Chapelle de Notre-Dame de Consolation of Paris, erected around 1900 in the grandiose French classical style.

Second Chicago Historical Society Building (1896)

NR

632 North Dearborn Street
Architect: Henry Ives Cobb

This building was the second permanent home of the Chicago Historical Society. Organized in 1856, when the city itself was only nineteen years old, the historical society purchased this site in 1865. Its first permanent building, designed by Burling & Whitehouse (see also 87), was completed there in 1868 and destroyed in the Chicago Fire three years later. Work on the present structure began in 1892. This rugged building is a handsome example of the Romanesque revival style made popular by H. H. Richardson (see 123). Its rough-hewn granite facade, rounded turrets with conical roofs, and bands of arched and transomed windows are typical of the style. The historical society was located here until 1931, when it moved to its present location in Lincoln Park (no. 97).

Medinah Temple (1912)   NR
Tree Studio   (1894)
Block bounded by Ontario Street, Wabash
    Avenue, Ohio and State streets
Architects of Medinah Temple: Huehl &
    Schmid, east half of block (1912)
Architects of Tree Studios: Parfitt Brothers,
    with Hill & Woltersdorf, west half of
    block (1894); Hill & Woltersdorf, Ohio
    and Ontario Street annexes (1912, 1913)

These two buildings seem to share little beyond their adja-
cency on the same city block. Yet in their origins they share
the same initial benefactor—Lambert Tree—who recog-
nized that works of art need a still, quiet, and serene place
in which to develop and that they also need a place where
they may be displayed and appreciated. The Tree Studio is
principally a place for the private search for artistic expres-

sion of painters, sculptors, architects, and designers—creators of the visual arts. The Medinah Temple is dedicated to performance, whether, because of its excellent acoustics, recording the Chicago Symphony Orchestra or in the late winter as the site for the Shrine Circus. The sedate profile of the Tree Studio reinforces its purpose, while the exuberant domes and highly textured surfaces of the Medinah Temple promise excitement, the unexpected, and the exotic to its audiences. Between them they fill their low-rise block with forms that are at human scale and visually diverse, providing an oasis of space and light in the increasingly dense high-rise development that surrounds them.

Montgomery Ward and Company (1907,   NR
1974)
618 West Chicago Avenue
Architects: Warehouse, Schmidt, Garden &
    Martin; Administration Building, 535
    West Chicago Avenue, Minoru Yamasaki
    & Associates

The warehouse was, at the time of its completion, the largest reinforced concrete structure in the world. The powerful horizontality of the long facade is strengthened by
projecting strips at the top and bottom of each spandrel.
Originally, the horizontal effect was more emphatic still,
since the brick facing of the spandrels was left unpainted
(now it is painted to match the concrete).

The concrete frame of the later Yamasaki administration building is sheathed in travertine.

Away from the Core

Chicago's reputation as a collection of neighborhoods of wide variety and assorted function as well as pronounced ethnic identities developed early and persists to day. To be sure, the city is not unique in these respects. In most American metropolises that took shape during the surging nineteenth century, the construction of transit lines encouraged citizens to move outward radially from a downtown business district, retaining access to the core but seeking either a residential setting closer to rural nature or a business environment more economically affordable.

Even so, Chicago negotiated this process in ways peculiar to itself. Its unparalleled rate of immigration during the late 1800s drove newly arrived inhabitants to cluster in exceptionally dense, tightly knit settlements. As the earlier subcultures thus established improved their lot, they tended to head toward the city's edges, leaving the less desirable spaces they had abandoned to poorer newcomers. The resultant pattern of sharp contrasts, both ethnic and economic, continues to the present day.

Over the years, the single natural feature that affected the formation of neighborhoods in Chicago was the lake front. Its continued impact is most obvious today in the ribbon of high-rise apartment buildings along Lake Shore Drive and in the townhouses of Astor Street, both districts marking the precincts of the more affluent—even as the city behind them still contains some of the most racially segregated and economically disadvantaged districts in the United States.

The land itself, however, is virtually flat and endless, of little historic consequence in differentiating one area from another. The river is narrow and easily bridged, more a thoroughfare for boats than a major natural divider. Neighborhoods have been organized less by topographical setting than by human decision, beginning with the Ordinance of 1787, which, before Chicago ever existed, had turned the Northwest Territory into a grid of mile-square parcels.

Upon that north-south grid the radial pattern of the transit lines was superimposed—again, one construct on another, independent of nature, operating as the chief determinants of Chicago's neighborhood growth. As early as 1869, the city's outward reach facilitated by the rail lines led planners to conceive a system of inland parks connected by boulevards that was meant as a far-flung public urban amenity, punctuating the sprawl of little houses that made up so much of the early inner city. The boulevards followed the grid in a giant U-shaped pattern extending from a point about 3 miles north of downtown westward about 4 miles, then southward about 10 miles and eastward again about 5 miles, rejoining the lake about 7 miles south of the core. Along this route six large parks ranging from two hundred to six hundred acres were laid out. Several other boulevards were also part of the 1869 plan and in the intervening years smaller parks have been added around the city. The six original greenswards still exist today in the form of Lincoln Park and Jackson Park, respectively anchoring the boulevard system at its north and south lake-front connections, and Humboldt, Garfield, Douglas, and Washington parks, these latter sited along the inland circuit. Similarly, enough of the boulevards remain—for example, Logan, Humboldt, Western, Garfield—that the entire original system may still be perceived.

This immense corporate exercise has done much to enliven the tableland of the Chicago cityscape. Unlike Manhattan, which is focused upon and dominated by Central Park, the Chicago system is decentralized, a fact that further reinforces the identities of the city's neighborhoods. In rather typical Chicago style, the motives behind the scheme stood for a mixture of conflict and cooperation between private interests and public aspiration: developers sought to raise the value of land around the parks and boulevards precisely because those additions enhanced the quality of ambient life. Citizens who could afford to live close to such space and greenery would thus secure the integrity of their neighborhoods, while the poor living at a distance could reach them by public transportation (presumably without threatening the comfortable neighborhoods). The fieldhouses in those parks functioned as mini–civic centers, providing sports, recreational, and even educational facilities to the people who used them.

Clearly, most of the map of Chicago is still made up of the streets that issue into and out of the parks and boulevards. Here, in the houses that line them, another local tradition is observable. In its earliest decades Chicago was widely known for its abundance of one-family dwellings, virtually all of them of frame construction. After so many were destroyed by the 1871 fire, apartment buildings often took their place, especially in areas closer to the core. Most of these were two- and three-flat freestanding structures with gabled roofs. Row houses are relatively uncommon in Chicago, where the standard lot width of 25 feet—a more generous dimension than is typical of the larger eastern American cities—encouraged a degree of sovereign, individualized space that seems in keeping with the city's decentralizing residential tendency. After the city limits expanded greatly around 1890, more and more houses of brick, sometimes

with stone facing, appeared. One of the most characteristic forms is the two- or three-flat building with a bay
window on its front, dining room and bedrooms amid-
ships, a kitchen and a porch to the rear, and a small yard
and a private garage facing the famous Chicago alley
that has provided the city a better delivery and garbage
collection system than that of many other American metropolises. To this house type, the product mostly of the
1900s and 1910s in such inner districts as Lakeview, West
Town, and Bridgeport, were added great quantities of
brick bungalows during postwar decades—the 1920s
and the 1950s—in more outlying areas like Norwood
Park, Austin, Berwyn, and Morgan Park. Commonplace
in South Shore and Edgewater is the courtyard apartment building, a form whose appearance in Oak Park
and Evanston as well proves that the formal boundaries
of Chicago in many places do little to distinguish suburban from city spaces.

Further to the congealment of individual residential
neighborhoods were the shopping centers that grew up
around the junctions of major streets (e.g., Lincoln and
Belmont, Cicero and Madison, and Seventy-ninth and
Stony Island). These clusters have lost much of their former vitality to the ubiquitous shopping malls within and
without the city, leaving Chicago neighborhoods to rely
for much of their remaining coherence on such institutions as the parish church, the public school, and the
local tavern, each of them cultivating as surely as cater-
ing to its own constituency. The frequent siting of the
church, for example, Holy Family, on a main thoroughfare tends to heighten the publicness of the parish, while
the elementary school, for example, Grover Cleveland
School, has often favored a side-street location, the better
to keep its children not only away from heavy traffic but
closer to home. The corner bar has traditionally occupied the ground floor of a typically small, freestanding
apartment building.

Notwithstanding these varying ongoing patterns, change remains constant. Even before the turn of the century the Germans and Scandinavians had moved north and northwest from their earliest locations closer in. The latter were taken up first by Poles, later by Hispanics. Old Jewish settlements on the West Side gradually became black during the 1950s and 1960s. Pilsen took its name from a Bohemian population that largely moved on to Berwyn and Cicero. A similar scenario has been repeated for numerous other ethnic groups and other parts of town. Several waves of immigration in the twentieth century, notably those that carried blacks north after World War I and Hispanics to the United States as a whole after World War II, have accelerated the moving about, altering the identities of ethnic groups associated with churches and schools (and taverns too). No agency meanwhile has had more of an effect on the fabric of the city in recent years than the motor car, which gave rise to the expressways of the 1950s and 1960s and divided neighborhoods physically and even spiritually, hastening the flight of the middle class to the suburbs.

The negative impact of many of these recent changes on the city's services cannot be overlooked in any discussion of Chicago's current urban condition. Until the crises that attach to education, law enforcement, and transportation are resolved, it is unlikely that substantial neighborhood growth and revitalization will occur. At the same time, recent efforts at gentrification have led to the takeover of some older districts (e.g., Printers' Row, North Clybourn Avenue) by younger professionals or to a nearly unprecedented intermingling of those newcomers with established ethnic groups (e.g., in Wicker Park and Ukrainian Village). Even altogether new neighborhoods have sprung up, like the constellations south of the Loop, some of them (e.g., Dearborn Park) having risen out of formerly deserted railroad yards. Here and there these areas, mostly financed by private interests, lie immediately adjacent to the city's more forlorn stretches; thus racial and class tensions vie with the hope that the new developments represent a measure of promise for attracting Chicago's lost populations back to the inner city.

Meanwhile, the vastness that stretches away from the core has been built as surely to serve industry and commerce as to provide for the residential needs of its population. Chicago's historic industrial prowess derived largely from the sprawling port facilities situated at its southern edge, while its rail lines enabled manufacturers and entrepreneurs to establish themselves on land sufficiently removed from the center to be cheap yet close enough to attract workers.

A telling example of the process is the growth of R. R. Donnelley and Sons, the largest printing plant in Chicago, which moved from its original home on Plymouth Court just south of the Loop (41) to its present, farther site at Twenty-third Street. The city's first industrial park, the Central Manufacturing District, was established by 1900 along Pershing Road near the old Stockyards. The rails were also integral to one of the most important architectural accomplishments of Chicago during its 1880–1900 golden age, the town of Pullman, which took shape about 15 miles southeast of downtown. There, following Chicago tradition, a private citizen, the railroad car manufacturer George Pullman, commissioned a young Chicago architect, Solon S. Beman, to conceive and assemble a totally planned community, much of which still stands.

The centrifugal process continues to affect industry, commerce, and entertainment as it has housing. It is the automobile, again taking the place of the railroad, that has moved on the aforementioned expressways ever outward, into the suburbs, while the two transportation systems have together effected the connection between downtown and airport facilities, chiefly O'Hare, that are necessarily located at or near the city's edge. Closer in but still distant from the Loop by as much as several miles are Chicago's huge convention and exposition center, McCormick Place, and its major sports arenas, Soldier Field, Comiskey Park, the Chicago Stadium, and Wrigley Field.

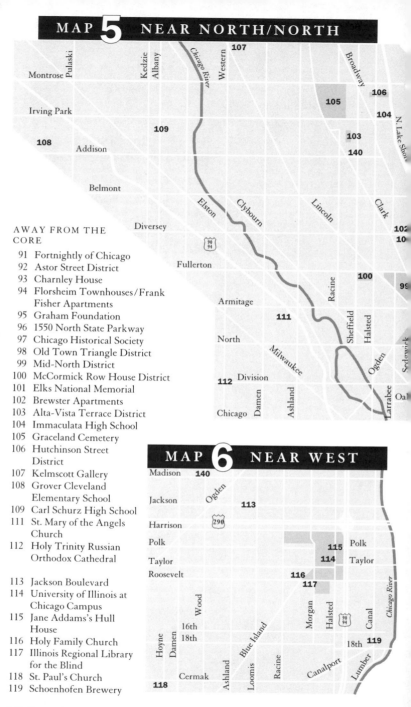

MAP 5 NEAR NORTH/NORTH

Montrose
Pulaski
Kedzie
Albany
Chicago River
Western
Broadway
107
106
105
104
Irving Park
N. Lake Shore
103
109
140
108
Addison
Belmont
Elston
Clybourn
Lincoln
Clark
Diversey
102
10
90 94
Fullerton
Racine
100
99
Armitage
111
Sheffield
Halsted
North
Milwaukee
Ogden
Sedgwick
112
Division
Oa
Chicago
Damen
Ashland
Larrabee

MAP 6 NEAR WEST

Madison **140**
Ogden
Jackson
113
Harrison
290
Polk
115 Polk
114
Taylor
Taylor
Roosevelt
116
117
Chicago River
Wood
16th
18th
Morgan
Halsted
Canal
90 94
Hoyne
Damen
Blue Island
18th **119**
Ashland
Loomis
Racine
Canalport
Lumber
Cermak
118

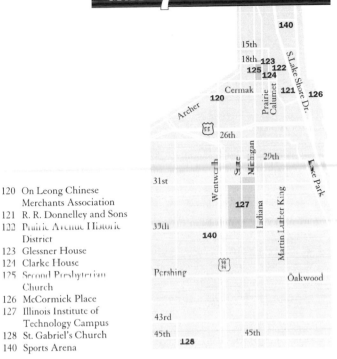

MAP 7 NEAR SOUTH

140

15th

18th **123**
125 **122**
124

Cermak
120   **121** **126**

Archer

26th

29th

31st

127

35th

140

Pershing   Oakwood

43rd

45th   45th
128

MAP 8 HYDE PARK

47th

49th   **129**

130

51st

131

53rd

132

134

55th

56th   **133**

57th

58th   **136**   **137**   **135**

59th

60th   MIDWAY PLAISANCE

JACKSON PARK

61st

Fortnightly of Chicago   (1892)   CL, NR
(Originally the Bryan Lathrop House)
120 East Bellevue Street
Architects: McKim, Mead & White

The unusually fine facade reflects the Georgian style of the
eighteenth century. The most memorable features include
the shallow relieving arches over the openings of the first
floor, the scale of their decoration, the subtle emphasis in
the two stringcourses and the cornice, and the vigor given
by the projection of the curved bays at each end of the
building. Two departures from Georgian tradition appear
in the asymmetrical entry and the elongated central window of the third floor. The latter was once adorned by a
light, openwork balcony. Similar balconies were also originally hung outside the three central windows of the second
floor.

Astor Street District   CL

North Astor Street between East Division
Street and East North Boulevard

Astor Street developed as the heart of Chicago's fashionable
Gold Coast area beginning in the 1880s. The earliest house
on the six-block street (named for John Jacob Astor) is the
large brick mansion at North Boulevard, designed by
Alfred F. Pashley in 1880 as the residence of the Catholic
Archbishop of Chicago. Still occupied by Chicago's arch
bishop, the house displays a lively profusion of bays, dormers, gables, and the chimneys typical of the Queen Anne
style. In 1882, Potter Palmer built his imposing residence,
designed by Cobb & Frost, demolished in 1950, on Lake
Shore Drive between Banks and Schiller streets, and soon
the area became as fashionable as Prairie Avenue had formerly been. During the next several decades, wealthy Chicagoans commissioned many prominent architects to design
townhouses along Astor and adjacent streets.

The largest house on Astor Street stands at the northwest corner of Burton and Astor. In 1892, *Chicago Tribune*
publisher Joseph Medill commissioned New York architect
Stanford White to design this finely proportioned example
of Renaissance revival as a wedding gift for his daughter
and son-in-law, the Robert W. Pattersons. Cyrus Hall Mc-
Cormick II, a later owner of the house, commissioned David Adler to design an addition to it on the north, more
than doubling its size. Adler's effort so precisely follows
that of White that it is barely distinguishable from the original structure.

Unlike the Patterson House, most other Astor Street
residences are compact, albeit substantial, townhouses.
Among the most notable are the James Charnley House at
1365 North Astor (93), by Adler & Sullivan; the neo-
Elizabethan James Houghteling houses at 1308–12 Astor,
designed by John Wellborn Root in 1887; the French Renaissance revival Joseph T. Ryerson House at 1406, designed

by David Adler in 1922; and the contemporary house at 1524, designed in 1968 by I. W. Colburn, which so completely respects its neighbors and the scale of the street.

Three Art Deco structures on the street date from the late 1920s and early 1930s: the Edward P. Russell House at 1444 Astor, designed by Holabird & Root in 1929, and two apartment buildings at 1301 and 1260, designed by Philip B. Maher in 1929 and 1930, respectively.

Apartment buildings had first appeared on Astor Street with Holabird & Roche's 1897 McConnell Apartments at 1210 Astor. This straightforward Chicago school structure is not unlike the commercial office buildings this firm was designing for downtown Chicago at the time, and it incorporates several similar features. It was not until the 1950s, however, that a proliferation of high-rise apartment buildings began to violate the scale of the area. Among these, Bertrand Goldberg's 1962 Astor Tower at 1300 Astor manages a measure of elegance, but most seem like clumsy giants next to their urbane late nineteenth- and early twentieth-century neighbors.

93

Charnley House (1892)   CL, NR
1365 North Astor Street
Architects: Adler & Sullivan

Although Frank Lloyd Wright contributed to this design
by Adler & Sullivan, documentary evidence and analysis of
the design and plan demonstrate the central role of Sullivan. Regardless of the pride of place in this collaboration,
this is among the finest city dwellings in Chicago, occupying a challenging site with assurance and taking full advan-
tage of its position at a jog in Astor Street as it intersects
Schiller Street. Orange Roman brick and finely cut limestone are the chief materials of the exterior. The interplay
of the severe block of the ground floor and the wooden
second-floor balcony contribute to the building's quality.
The entry vestibule leads up a few steps to a cross hall and
the seemingly vertiginous staircase. The building was restored in the late 1980s by John Eifler of Skidmore, Owings
& Merrill. The Seymour H. Persky Foundation gave the
Charmley House to the Society of Architectural Historians
for its use as their national headquarters in 1995.

94

Florsheim Townhouses (1937)
1328 North State Parkway
Frank Fisher Apartments (1938)
1209 North State Parkway
Architect: Andrew N. Rebori

These two small buildings are examples of the Art Moderne style that flourished during the 1930s. Curved windows that wrap around rounded corners and the extensive use of glass blocks, then a new material, give a "streamlined" look to buildings of this style. The ornament and textured treatment of the brick are not characteristic of the style but add visual interest. The long, narrow courtyards provide light, air, and a measure of privacy to the buildings, while Rebori's fresh use of simple materials reflects one of his greatest strengths.

Graham Foundation for Advanced Studies in the Fine Arts (1902)   CL, NR
(Originally Madlener House)
4 West Burton Place
Architect: Richard E. Schmidt

The clear, cubical mass of this building is as forceful as a Florentine palace, but in its exterior detailing it is clearly related to the Prairie style made popular by Frank Lloyd Wright. The design of this house was a close collaboration between Richard Schmidt and his then draftsman and later partner, Hugh Garden. A strong emphasis on the horizontal is apparent in the base, the stringcourses, and the grouping of the windows. The decoration around the door is a fine example of modern ornament, similar to Sullivan's geometric type. Garden called his ornament "gardenesque." The interior, notable for the richness of its woods, was remodeled and restored for the Graham Foundation by Brenner, Danforth & Rockwell. John Vinci has recently transformed the side yard of the building into a garden of architectural fragments of demolished Chicago buildings.

1550 North State Parkway (1912)
Architects: Marshall & Fox

This elegant apartment building was designed by a firm
noted for its luxury hotels and apartments. Benjamin Marshall and Charles E. Fox practiced together from 1905 until
Fox's death in 1926. During that time they designed the
Blackstone Hotel (1909; 1) and the Blackstone Theater (60
East Balbo; 1911), the apartment building at 999 North
Lake Shore Drive (1912), the Edgewater Beach Hotel
(1916; demolished 1969), the Drake Hotel (1920; 78), and
the John B. Murphy Memorial (1926; 87). The building at
1550 originally had a single fifteen-room apartment per

floor. The principal living rooms—a central "petit salon" flanked on one side by the "grand salon" with a rounded bay and on the other by a dining room and "orangerie"—were arranged along the north side of the building, overlooking Lincoln Park. This provided a continuous sequence of formal spaces over 100 feet long. The bedrooms spanned the east side of the building and enjoyed a view of the lake. The kitchen, service rooms, and servants' quarters were located at the southwest section of the building. The enormous, high-ceilinged apartments and dignified Beaux-Arts facade facing Lincoln Park have made this one of Chicago's elite apartment building addresses.

97

Chicago Historical Society (1931, 1971, 1988)
North Clark Street at North Avenue
Architects: Graham, Anderson, Probst & White; additions by Alfred Shaw & Associates (1971), Holabird & Root (1988)

In its third incarnation, the Chicago Historical Society (see 88) was a red-brick Georgian revival building that had the southwest corner of Lincoln Park to itself. In 1971 the first of two large additions was attached along the full length of the original west elevation. It was widely criticized for its heavy-handed mixture of modernism with neoclassicism, and in 1988 it was replaced, or more exactly covered over, by a larger and longer tract. This last structure, now called the Daniel F. and Ada L. Rice Pavilion, contains the main entrance to the building, on the Clark Street side. While it is intrinsically superior to the first addition in its lively juxtaposition of a red-brick facade with a hi-tech frontispiece and a two-story-high curved glass wall at the south end, it is nearly as stylistically unrelated to the old Georgian building as its predecessor was.

98

Old Town Triangle District   CL, NR
Bounded roughly by North Avenue, Lincoln
    Park, and the extension of Ogden Avenue
    north of Armitage Avenue

This distinctive area was settled in the 1850s primarily by working-class German families who built modest frame houses of the type now known as "Chicago cottages." The Chicago cottage could be built quickly and easily because it employs a balloon frame, an innovative structural system developed in Chicago in the 1830s. Instead of the heavy timber posts and beams secured by mortise-and-tenon joints that formed the traditional wooden frame, the balloon frame used ready-cut lumber and machine-made nails. The Chicago cottage is usually either 1½ or 2½ stories high, with a pitched roof and gable ends at front and rear. It usually has a high basement and a raised front entrance placed next to a pair of windows. Usually quite plain but occasionally decorated, these structures continued to be built in the area until an 1874 fire ordinance prohibited construction of frame buildings within the city limits. Later many row houses were built in the area, usually either Italianate or Queen Anne in style. A row of five houses at 1826–34 North Lincoln Park West was designed by Louis Sullivan and completed in 1885. Old Town experienced a period of decline earlier in this century, but in the late 1940s one of the earliest neighborhood revitalization efforts in this country began there. During the past thirty years, many houses in Old Town have been rehabilitated, and the scale and charm of the neighborhood have been preserved.

Mid-North District

Bounded generally by Fullerton Avenue,
Clark Street, Armitage Avenue, and
Lincoln Avenue and Orchard Street

Fullerton Avenue was the northern boundary of Chicago
when Mid-North began to develop as a residential area
around the middle of the nineteenth century. The fire that
destroyed the city in 1871 died out in this vicinity because
here the frame houses were more widely separated than
those closer to the river. Three of the four houses in Mid-
North that survived the fire still stand: the Policeman Bel-
linger cottage at 2121 North Hudson Street, and the two
houses at 2339 and 2343 North Cleveland. After the fire,
brick row houses and freestanding residences were built,
giving Mid-North the late-nineteenth-century urban character that still prevails. Within the district, the double-
bayed house at 440 West Belden was designed by Louis Sullivan in 1883, as was 2147 Cleveland in 1884. Mid-North
also has a large number of contemporary structures that are
sympathetic in scale and materials to the older buildings.

100

McCormick Row House
District (1882–89)   CL
Between Belden and Fullerton avenues,
    Halsted Street, and the elevated tracks
Architect: A. M. F. Colton & Son

These brick row houses were built as rental units to supple-
ment the endowment of McCormick Theological Seminary.
Founded in Indiana in 1829 as the Indiana Theological
Seminary, this Presbyterian institution moved to Chicago
thirty years later with the promise of financial assistance
from Cyrus Hall McCormick, inventor of the reaper. Construction of the campus began in 1862, although the row
houses were not built until twenty years later. The houses
fronting on Belden and Fullerton avenues were the first
constructed. They are a simplified Queen Anne style with a
varied roof line, ornamental brickwork, and contrasting
stone trim. The houses facing away from these and fronting
on Chalmers Place, a quiet street bordering a small private
park, were built in the late 1880s. These later houses are
quite severe: cleanly incised window openings and deeply
recessed door openings are set simply into the broad facade.

which is of brown brick trimmed in brown stone. A symmetrical arrangement of round and triangular gables marks the roof line. In 1973, McCormick Seminary left its North Side campus to affiliate with the theological schools at the University of Chicago. The row houses were then sold to private owners and the institutional buildings were acquired by DePaul University.

101

Elks National Memorial Building   (1926)
2750 Lakeview Avenue
Architects: Main building, Egerton
   Swartwout; Magazine Building, Holabird
   & Root (1967)

The central, dominating unit of the structure is a massive cylinder surmounted by a flattened dome, 100 feet above the floor level. The building is encircled by a stately, 38-foot-high colonnade that rises from a belting frieze carved in high relief. Entered by a single arched doorway, this central building constitutes the memorial feature of the edifice.

Sculptures are by Adolph A. Weinman, James Earle Fraser, and Laura Gardin Fraser, with murals by Edwin H. Blashfield and Eugene Savage.

Brewster Apartments (1893)   CL
2800 North Pine Grove
Architect: Enoch Hill Turnock

The narrow windows and the rough-faced quartzite blocks
of the wall make the Brewster in its external appearance a
rather traditional and somewhat romanticized version of
the oriel windowed apartment buildings of the Chicago
school. The interior design, however, represents a bold solution to the problem of admitting natural light to the
spaces inside the building. In plan it is a hollow rectangle,
the inner court of which is surmounted by a gabled skylight—a common form for the multistory office block in
the nineteenth century, but one which posed a peculiar dif-
ficulty in the case of an apartment building. To provide ac-

cess to upper-floor apartments from a single centrally
located elevator, Turnock introduced a little pedestrian
bridge running the length of the court in each floor, with
lateral branches extending to the individual entrance doors.
The bridge decks are composed of glass blocks supported
by light steel girders at the edges. The thin frames of these
translucent bridges and the open grillwork of the elevator
shaft form a vivid pattern of black lines set off against the
diffused light falling from the glass roof above the court.

103

Alta Vista Terrace District (1900–1904)   CL, NR
One-block-long street, running north-south,
    located at 3800 north and 1050 west
Architect: J. C. Brompton

Alta Vista Terrace is composed of forty masonry row
houses, twenty on each side of the block-long street that
runs from Grace Street on the south to Byron Street on the
north. Each unit, built with brick party walls 18 inches
thick, is situated on a lot approximately 24 feet wide and 40
feet deep, creating the effect of a continuous facade on each

side of the terrace, which is approximately 480 feet long. The buildings are particularly noteworthy for their unity of scale.

The facades reflect adaptations of various architectural styles. In what were originally the twenty different Roman-brick facades of the forty houses are to be found such divergent architectural motifs as Doric and Ionic wood pilasters, flamboyant Gothic arches, Palladian windows, stained- and leaded-glass fanlights, bay and bow windows, sheet-metal cornices at roof levels, and a wealth of mold-ings, brackets, dentils, festoons, and other classic details. The false half-timbering is a later modification.

104

Immaculata High School (1922)   CL, NR
600 West Irving Park Road
Architect: Barry Byrne

The architect, an early and important student of Frank Lloyd Wright, studied at Wright's Oak Park studio from 1902 until 1908. This building is L-shaped in plan, with the hollow housing the entry and facing southwest on Irving Park Road. The walls are brown tapestry brick with limestone trim, and the roof is red tile with low, unusually shaped, copper-clad dormers. Windows are banked vertically under pointed arches. The limestone canopy and statue of the Virgin at the front entrance are the work of Alfonso Iannelli, who worked frequently with Byrne and also with Wright, having, for example, designed the sculpture at Wright's Midway Gardens (demolished 1929). The statue was removed by its current owner, the American Islamic College. Byrne also designed two additions, a convent in 1955 and a western extension of the school in 1956.

105

Hutchinson Street District   CL
Hutchinson Street between Marine Drive
    and Hazel Street

These two blocks contain a unique concentration of houses designed by George Maher. Maher is frequently classified as a Prairie school architect, although his designs are highly eclectic and employ forms borrowed from various architectural idioms. The first house Maher designed here was built in 1894 at the northeast corner of Hutchinson and Hazel. It is a picturesque Queen Anne house with a lively profusion of projecting bays, porches, and turrets.

Maher's house at 826 Hutchinson Street was built in 1904. Its broad horizontal lines and formal composition demonstrate the influence of Frank Lloyd Wright's early work. Maher's most impressive design on the street is the house built in 1913 at 817. It displays a Prairie school horizontality, has long bands of windows, and demonstrates Maher's "motif-rhythm theory," which calls for the repetition of a single decorative element throughout a design to create unity. The house at 750 Hutchinson was also designed by Maher in 1902 and has a front door set into a stone frame that is reminiscent of the design of Louis Sullivan's Wainwright Tomb in St. Louis. The Hutchinson Street District contains several other excellent houses built around the turn of the century. The nicely massed and finely detailed house at 4234 Hazel Street, built in 1904, was designed by William Drummond for the office of Richard Schmidt. Both of these architects are grouped with the Prairie school.

106

Graceland Cemetery (1860–)
Block bounded by Irving Park Road, Clark
Street, Montrose Avenue, and the C.T.A.
elevated railroad tracks

Since the chosen burial ground of Chicago's social and professional elite has long been Graceland Cemetery, it is not
surprising that it is the most touristically inviting graveyard
in the city. It is also visually the most arresting. While visitors flock there to view the final resting places of people
with names like Field, Palmer, Schoenhofen, Armour, and
McCormick, the great commercial builders of the city, they
find monuments to these families that have been created in
many cases by the comparably illustrious architectural
builders of the city.

Thus the mastaba-like tomb of Martin Ryerson and
the elegantly decorated mausoleum of Carrie Eliza Getty

were designed by Louis Sullivan, while George Pullman's remains repose beneath a single lofty Corinthian column by Solon S. Beman. Some of the architects themselves are memorialized by their colleagues: John Wellborn Root by Charles Atwood and Jules Wegman of D. H. Burnham & Co., Sullivan himself by Thomas Tallmadge (and others), Ludwig Mies van der Rohe by his grandson Dirk Lohan.

Chicago's most famous early twentieth-century sculptor Lorado Taft is responsible for the figure of Death that guards the tomb of Dexter Graves.

Among the many other notables buried in Graceland are the boxers Jack Johnson and Bob Fitzsimmons, baseball magnate William Hulbert (note the baseball-shaped tomb stone!), the newspaper publishers Victor Lawson and Joseph Medill, the statesmen Governor John P. Altgeld and

Mayor Carter H. Harrison, and the designer-educator who revived the Bauhaus in Chicago, László Moholy-Nagy. The body of early Chicago architect William LeBaron Jenney lies in an unmarked grave in the Jenney family plot.

Horace W. S. Cleveland's early plan of the cemetery, dating from the 1860s, was later revised and enlarged by Ossian Simonds. Paths and roadways are laid out in the informal, curvilinear manner true to the mid-nineteenth-century romantic vision of the communal cemetery as a nature-bound retreat rather than the traditional, tightly composed churchyard. The largest plots, belonging to the most renowned of the deceased, are grouped around an artificial lake, Willowmere, near the northern boundary of the cemetery.

The service buildings at Graceland, including the crematorium and the original part of the chapel, were designed by Holabird & Roche.

107

Kelmscott Gallery (1922)   CL
(Originally Krause Music Store)
4611 North Lincoln Avenue
Architects: Louis H. Sullivan and William
   C. Presto

This small store is the product of a minor architect, but the design of its facade was the last commission received by Louis Sullivan. Certain elements, notably the restrained ornament in the recessed entryway and the sensitive patterning of the upper wall, are typical of Sullivan's finest work. On the other hand, the three large ornamental forms that appear on the center line of the facade seem hung on rather than integrated with the design as a whole. They overwhelm the little facade, which is far too short to carry such an emphatic central emphasis.

Carl Schurz High School   (1909)   CL
Milwaukee Avenue at Addison Street
Architect: Dwight H. Perkins

This school building is a dramatic composition of rising
verticals in the walls, suddenly stopped by the deep over-
hangs of high-pitched roofs set at various levels. A very
strong stringcourse at the top of the first floor echoes the
roof line. The building is fronted by a great lawn that
makes it handsomely and comprehensively visible from
Milwaukee Avenue. Later wings by other architects followed Perkins's design very well. The 1994 cleaning by Ross-
Barney & Jankowski reveals a stunning polychromatic richness in the building, hidden under years of grime, and
demonstrates Perkins's interest in interlocking forms.

109

Grover Cleveland Elementary
School (1910)
3850 North Albany Street
Architect: Dwight H. Perkins

Here Perkins has conceived a strong, severe, persuasive design, the chief forms emphasized by borders of contrasting brick. The piers, which seem like abstractions of Gothic buttresses, terminate in interesting capital blocks, an effective transition to the wall above. (By a curious optical illusion these piers seem wider at the second and third stories than at the first, perhaps because of their lighter color.)

Chicago O'Hare International
Airport (1963–)

Northwest far city limits, junction of
  Northwest Tollway and Tri-State Tollway
Architects: Naess & Murphy; C. F. Murphy
  Associates; Murphy/Jahn; Perkins & Will;
  O'Hare Associates; Control Tower: I.M.Pei (1963–);
  Holmes and Narver (1995–)

In terms of traffic one of the several busiest airports in the
world, O'Hare is a mammoth enterprise that has grown
steadily since it opened in 1963. Most phases of design have
been supervised by the same architectural firm, which has
changed its name from Naess & Murphy to C. F. Murphy
Associates and finally to Murphy/Jahn. On the other hand,
the most recent addition, the International Terminal, is the
work of another Chicago office, Perkins & Will.

    The chief designer of the earliest terminals (now called
2 and 3), together with their attached concourses, the heating and refrigeration plant and various service buildings,
was Stanislav Gladych. Gertrude Kerbis was responsible for

the restaurant that connects the terminals. Recognizably Miesian in their lean, rectilinear steel-and-glass geometry, these structures lent a consistency of appearance to O'Hare that continued with the addition of the O'Hare Hotel (chief designer John Novack) to the complex in 1972.

With the completion of an immense, 7000-car parking garage (chief designer Gladych) in the same year, 1972, O'Hare reached the end of its first phase, following which a new generation of taste became manifest. Terminal 1, designed by Helmut Jahn, retains the old Chicago tradition of expressive use of the frame structure, most obvious in the folded roof trusses of the pavilion and the vaults that cover the lofty parallel concourses B and C. Otherwise, however, the new building is an example of the hi-tech manner at its most cheerfully aggressive.

Color, assigned an especially lively role in Terminal 1, is most noticeable at the underground level, where the B and C concourses are connected by a moving walkway. This 800-foot-long tunnel is enlivened by variegated corrugated glass walls and an overhead neon sculpture by Michael Hayden. The whole ensemble is further brightened by a contemporary musical soundtrack, its first form created by William Kraft, its later one by Gary Fry.

Color is also an important expressive feature of another underground architectural component of the O'Hare complex. It is the last stop, the O'Hare station, on the public transit rail line that runs on the median strip of the John F. Kennedy Expressway, an eight-lane artery connecting the airport directly with downtown Chicago. The most notable feature of the station, which was designed by Helmut Jahn in 1984, is a tall wall of backlit, gold-illuminated glass brick flanking the track beds. It is articulated in a vertical rhythm of alternating ridges and grooves akin to that of the walls in the aforementioned connecting tunnel of Terminal 1.

The latest addition to O'Hare, one of the largest and most ambitious parts of the airport, is the International

Terminal, designed by Ralph Johnson of Perkins & Will and scheduled for opening in 1993.

Chicago's position as a major connecting point in global travel necessitated not only this project but its formidable capacity of one million square feet. Its location adjacent to the principal entrance route to O'Hare and in front, or east, of the main mass of buildings makes it the first airport structure visible to motorists arriving from the city, as well as to travelers coming from abroad.

The building is composed of three levels, two of the lower ones given over to arrival facilities, baggage handling and related services. The top level is the most auspicious, a generously proportioned, boldly structured departure hall, a veritable galleria, whose curvilinear roof admits ample natural light. The plan is roughly crescent-shaped, with concourses arranged along the outer curved edge and extending outward from the terminal, like two great arms.

The various facilities at O'Hare have expanded over so large an area that an automated rail transit system has been designed by O'Hare Associates with Murphy/Jahn to move passengers from place to place in the airport complex, notably between the new International Terminal and the older terminals, the main parking garage, and the remote parking lots.

111

St. Mary of the Angels Church (1920)
1850 North Hermitage
Architects: Worthmann & Steinbach;
    restoration by Holabird & Root (1992)

One of the most ambitious of Chicago's many neighborhood churches, St. Mary of the Angels reflects a strong influence from the Roman High Renaissance. Its most compelling external element is a dome, reportedly modeled after the rotunda Michelangelo designed for St. Peters in Rome. A five-aisled interior, one of the most capacious

among Chicago churches, features a barrel-vaulted nave that meets the transept at the crossing, where the dome, resting on pendentives, rises to a height of 135 feet above the floor. Built for Polish immigrants, St. Mary enjoyed its most prosperous years between 1920 and 1950. Later demographic changes have led a variety of ethnic groups, chiefly Latinos, as well as urban professionals from Bucktown and Wicker Park, to share the church with its original Polish congregation.

Gradual deterioration of the structure necessitated its closing in 1987, but a program of renovation, supervised by Holabird & Root, has given back to it much of its handsome original condition. The stained glass windows, many of them designed by the Zettler atelier in Munich, have been restored by Rigalli Studios of Chicago. The church reopened in 1992.

112

Holy Trinity Russian Orthodox Cathedral   CL, NR
(1903)
1121 North Leavitt Street
Architect: Louis H. Sullivan

The cathedral is interesting as a work in a traditional guise by an architect normally associated with more modern building types. The basic form is that of Russian churches derived from earlier Byzantine architecture. The central plan is treated as a square with extensions at ground level, its central space crowned with a dome. The interior is small, but with relatively large arches. The shallow dome and the painted decoration combine to produce an effect of delicacy and refinement, as of a richly decorated coffer or jewel box. The exterior is simple, with occasional exotic touches in curved shapes or angular window hoods. The onion-shaped spire above the lantern was inspired by the bulbous domes found in Russian church architecture. Ornament, otherwise sparingly used, is most striking in the cut-out treatment of the sheet metal canopy over the entrance.

113

Jackson Boulevard District CL

1500 block of West Jackson Boulevard

This block of houses typifies the pleasant environment of the Near West Side when that area was a fashionable residential community at the end of the nineteenth century. Ornamental details of the architectural styles popular during the period of the street's development—Italianate, Queen Anne, and Richardsonian Romanesque—abound intact. The most prominent resident of the street was Carter Henry Harrison, who served as mayor of Chicago for five terms beginning in 1879 and lived in a house at Jackson and Ashland that has since been demolished. Benjamin F. Ferguson, a benefactor of the Art Institute, lived at 1501 Jackson Boulevard for a time.

114

University of Illinois at Chicago (1965–)

Generally bounded by Harrison, Halsted,
Taylor, and Morgan streets

Architects: General Plan: Skidmore,
Owings & Merrill, Walter Netsch design partner

Initially intended as a great public undergraduate university to serve students from the metropolitan region who were expected to commute to school, the campus is sited near a series of intersections of major road and rail transportation links. The faculty and students were then expected to circulate rather like automobiles, with high-level express walkways and grade-level local walks. At the center of the campus was a complex of lecture halls and open spaces described as an intellectual agora. To pull all this together, Walter Netsch used the geometries of his field theory, which he believed would provide a comprehensive sense of order for the students at what was understood to be a very large complex. The practical and symbolic merits of this plan were so thoroughly disputed that in 1994 the raised walkways and central space were removed in an effort to make the campus more familiar.

115

Jane Addams's Hull House and Dining   CL, NR
Hall (1856)
800 South Halsted Street
Architect unknown: house constructed 1856;
   dining hall, Pond & Pond, architects
   (1905); restoration and reconstruction,
   Frazier, Raftery, Orr & Fairbank,
   architects (1967).

These buildings are all that remain of the most famous social settlement in the United States. In 1856, Charles Hull
built this Italianate residence in what was then a suburban
area just southwest of downtown Chicago. Hull left the
house a dozen years later, and by the 1880s it was surrounded by factories and tenements. In 1889, Jane Addams
and Ellen Gates Starr rented several rooms in the house

and started a social settlement to aid the urban poor, particularly the large immigrant population in the immediate vicinity. As the settlement expanded its programs, additional space was needed. The veranda and cupola were removed from the house, and a third floor was added. Gradually, twelve additional structures (including the residents' dining hall that remains), all designed by Irving and Allen Pond, were built around the Hull residence so that the original structure was barely visible.

After Addams's death in 1935, the Hull House Association continued her work at the settlement until the early 1960s, when the property was acquired for construction of a new campus of the University of Illinois. The association at that time decided to decentralize its activities throughout the city. With the exception of the dining hall, which was moved about 200 yards from its original site, all the buildings surrounding the original house were demolished. The third-floor addition to the house was removed, the cupola and veranda recreated, and the house restored as a memorial to Jane Addams.

116

Holy Family Church (1857–74)
1076 West Roosevelt Road
Architects: John M. Van Osdel; Dillenburg
& Zucher; Julius Huber
St. Ignatius College Prep School (1867–69)
1072 West Roosevelt Road
Architects: Toussaint Menard and others

The oldest Jesuit church in Chicago, Holy Family is mostly
Gothic in style, although the corbel tables on the facade are
suggestive of the Romanesque. The exterior by Dillenburg
& Zucher is faced with yellow brick, while Van Osdel's interior features powerful compound piers that have settled—
stably—as much as 18 inches out of plumb. Especially notable is the program of stained glass windows, the best of
them dating from 1907 and executed by the Von Gehrich-
ten Art Glass Company of Columbus, Ohio. Earlier still, in
fact the oldest extant stained glass windows in Chicago, are
those in the clerestory. They were designed and installed in
1860 by the W. H. Carse Company of Chicago.

General deterioration forced the church to close in 1984. A massive reconstruction program has begun, and reopening is anticipated in 1995. The supervising architect is John Vinci. Restoration of elements in the interior is credited to Patrick J. Caddle for the statuary, to Robert Furhoff for the stencils on the walls of the aisles.

St. Ignatius, to the east, is modeled somewhat naively after the Second Empire style popular in America following the Civil War. The building conveys a simple force and energy on the exterior, while the interior contains some of the most impressive spaces that have survived from pre-fire Chicago. The tall ceilings and the overall axiality contribute to a handsomely formal effect that has been preserved or enhanced in the course of several later additions and renovations, the latest supervised by the school's president, Rev. Donald Rowe and carried out by an assortment of architects in the course of the 1980s. The grandest space is the Brunswick Room on the top floor. Designed by an unknown architect in 1888 and recently restored to its original condition, it is a balconied library most notable for its elegantly carved wood. Elsewhere in the building many old stencils have been restored while new ones, designed specially by Robert Furhoff and executed in 1990, add a winning embellishment to the main working library.

117

Illinois Regional Library for the Blind and Physically Handicapped (1978)
1055 West Roosevelt Road
Architect: Stanley Tigerman as consultant
   to Jerome R. Butler, Jr., City Architect

This building houses a state distribution center for Braille library materials, as well as a citywide library for the blind and physically handicapped, and, on the second floor, a local branch of the Chicago Public Library. Circulation areas in the interior are marked by linear plans and built-in furnishings which are easily memorized so that blind users

can maneuver conveniently. Directly inside the west wall is the circulation corridor, defined by a long counter that curves inward at each of four service desks so that a user can, as he approaches it, move out of the main aisle. The curving corridor is reflected on the exterior by a whimsical undulating window set into the concrete wall. The lower part of the window enables someone in a wheel chair to look inside, while the higher points are opposite the service desks so that library personnel can see out.

The architect intended paradoxes throughout the design. The lightweight baked enamel panels are made to seem heavy, since they are only infrequently opened by the insertion of small windows. On the other hand, the structural concrete wall is broken by the undulating window, which amounts to so long and sustained an incision that the rampart it is part of seems curiously insubstantial. Because of a tri-level arrangement of the stacks, the smaller exterior elements are three stories high, and the larger elements are only two stories. At the same time, the structure is brightly colored, with structural parts painted yellow, mechanical ducts and electrical and plumbing conduits blue, the metal wall panels red. It also offers a vivid contrast to the drab surrounding and enlivens a structure that serves a very serious purpose.

St. Paul Church (1897–99)
2234 South Hoyne
Architect: Henry J. Schlacks

Schlacks, one of the most prolific church architects in Chi
cago, was competent in a striking assortment of historical
styles. St. Paul ranks among his finest local efforts. Commissioned by a German parish on the near southwest side,
the building is remarkable for its well-crafted use of brick,
a material common to German Gothic architecture of the
Middle Ages. Indeed the siting of the church, its twin towers hovering over the small factories and low houses of its
immediate vicinity, brings to mind a medieval setting even
today. The interior is also noteworthy for its brickwork,
and no less for its colorful program of mosaics, especially
over the chancel arch.

Schoenhofen Brewery Building (1902)   CL, NR
West 18th Street and Canalport (NE corner)
Architects: Richard E. Schmidt; Hugh
    Garden

This is a characteristic example of the work of the group of
Chicago's architects who were developing a nonhistorical
approach at the beginning of the century. It demonstrates a
fine appreciation of the qualities of brick as both a building
and a decorative material. No less noteworthy are the proportioning, the detailing, and the lettering of the powerful
arched entrance.

Although Schmidt was the commissioned architect,
the design was apparently made by Hugh Garden, who
was retained by Schmidt for occasional projects prior to
1906, the year they formed a partnership.

Recent restorations have returned the building to a
faithful approximation of its original appearance.

120

On Leong Chinese Merchants Association (1927)
2216 South Wentworth Avenue
Architects: Michaelsen & Rognstad

This brick-and-terra-cotta-clad structure was built as the
headquarters of a Chinese-American businessman's association dating from the early twentieth century. The two fan-
ciful pagodas, the elaborately canopied entrance, the upper
arcades, and the colorful ornament are the primary elements of the design. The building and the entrance arch to
the north reflect ethnic pride and serve as an appropriate
entrance to Chicago's Chinatown.

R. R. Donnelley and Sons Company Building (1912)

350 East 22d Street
Architects: Howard Van Doren Shaw (1912,
1917, 1924); Charles Z. Klauder (1931)

When the Donnelley Company outgrew its printing plant
on Plymouth Court (41), the same architect was commissioned to design this new plant. Like its predecessor, it is an
excellent industrial building. In both, Shaw employed traditional forms in highly original ways. Here the facade is
more straightforward: broad piers define wide rectangular
bays, and carefully proportioned spandrels and windows
create a uniform rhythm from bottom to top. Gothic elements are employed extensively, from the buttressed corner
tower to the limestone trim. The ornament incorporates
emblems of early printers.

122

Prairie Avenue Historic District   CL, NR
South Prairie, South Michigan, and South
   Indiana avenues, between 18th and 19th
   streets

From the 1870s through the end of the nineteenth century, many of Chicago's prominent merchants, manufacturers, and businessmen—including Marshall Field, Philip D. Armour, George B. Pullman, and John J. Glessner—lived in imposing residences along Prairie Avenue on the city's near South Side. Later the area declined and most of the grand houses were demolished. Those that are left recall much of the elegance of that era and in several respects are unique in the Chicago scene. They form the substance of the Prairie Avenue Historic District created by the Chicago Architectural Foundation and the City of Chicago.

The cornerstone of the district is the Glessner House (123), the sole remaining building in Chicago by H. H. Richardson, one of the most distinguished figures in American architectural history. Directly across the street from the Glessner House is the William W. Kimball House, at 1801 South Prairie, designed in 1892 by Solon S. Beman, in his own right the player of a major role in the shaping of the early Chicago cityscape. With its handsomely articulated sloped roofs, corbel-topped chimneys and copper-clad finials, the Kimball House is probably the best extant example of the French chateau style in the city.

Along Prairie Avenue south of these two residences are a couple of other relics of the district's halcyon days. The Coleman Ames House, at 1811 South Prairie, built in 1886 by two well-remembered Chicago architects, Henry Ives Cobb and Charles Sumner Frost, is perceptibly indebted to Richardson, while the earliest of the old residences on the avenue, built in the early 1870s, the Elbridge Keith House, is an anonymous effort in the Italianate style. Two other buildings located on nearby streets but considered part of the Prairie Avenue Historic District are the charming, century-and-a-half-old Henry B. Clarke House (124) and the splendidly decorated Second Presbyterian Church (125).

Earlier plans for an outdoor park space between the Glessner House and the Clarke House, to be filled with architectural fragments, have been replaced by a program of notably more far-reaching preservationist significance. Foundation stones representing the outlines of the lost houses along Prairie Avenue between Eighteenth and Nineteenth streets will be laid down on their original sites, and the area between the Glessner House and the Clarke House will be landscaped to simulate the character of that space as it would have appeared in the 1870s and 1880s.

123

Glessner House (1887)   CL, NR
1800 South Prairie Avenue
Architect: Henry Hobson Richardson

Two of Richardson's finest designs were realized in Chicago: the Marshall Field Wholesale Store and the John J. Glessner House, both finished in 1887. The former was razed in 1930 and the latter was saved from demolition in 1966 only by the concerted efforts of a group of private citizens led by several architects, including Harry Weese and Ben Weese of Chicago and Philip Johnson of New York. Thus the Glessner House has been not only a standing architectural treasure but an arena of the ongoing preservationist debate of the last two decades.

Richardson's creative habits often favored the use of

heavy rusticated masonry forms reminiscent of the Romanesque period. He employed this approach consciously and emphatically in the Glessner House, since his client desired a residence that conveyed an image of enduring strength. And so it does, with its expanse of powerful walls of layered ashlar, its massive arches, and its overall spareness of ornament.

In the interior, however, a contrasting warmth and intimacy appropriate to the privacy of its inhabitants are perceptible in generously scaled spaces dressed in rich dark woods. Richardson was not content to entrust the interior to assistants, but rather supervised it himself. He also actively persuaded the Glessners to share his taste for the Arts and Crafts movement, the influence of which is apparent in the decorative program of the house.

Following its rescue from destruction in 1966, the house became the property of the Chicago School of Architecture Foundation, later the Chicago Architecture Foundation, which still owns it and which has steadily pursued a program of preservation. Thirteen rooms have been restored to their original state, although one space on the second floor, a conference room, was remodeled in 1976 in the contemporary manner by Hammond, Beeby & Babka. The courtyard, which was once sloped to accommodate vehicular traffic, has been leveled, also in the 1970s, but plans for the restoration of the incline, as well as other components of the house and its dependencies, are on the drawing boards.

124

Clarke House (1836)   CL, NR
1855 South Indiana Avenue
Architect: Unknown

The singularity of the Henry B. Clarke House is that it is the oldest building still standing in Chicago. Its eastern portico and the original tall window shutters have been restored, showing proportions typical of the Greek revival.

The spaciousness of the earliest ambitious homes of the city is suggested by the triple-sashed windows, which attest to the high-ceilinged rooms within.

Shortly after the Fire of 1871 the Widow Clarke House, as it is sometimes called, was moved from its original site near Sixteenth Street and Michigan Avenue. For many years it stood at Forty-fifth Street and Wabash Avenue and served as a meeting hall for a church. It has now been returned, as part of the Prairie Avenue Historic District, to a location close to the original one.

125

Second Presbyterian Church (1874)   CL, NR
1936 South Michigan Avenue
Architect: James Renwick; remodeled by
    Howard Van Doren Shaw, 1901

James Renwick of New York was one of the foremost
American practitioners of the Gothic revival style. This
church suffered a fire in 1900, following which Howard
Van Doren Shaw designed a new interior and modified the
exterior. He altered the fenestration by replacing Renwick's
pointed-arch clerestory windows with simple rectangular

ones and the rose window above the entrance with an opening crowned by a pointed arch. He also lowered the ridge of the roof.

Perhaps the most opulent features of the church are the art glass windows of the main sanctuary. Seven of these, including the one over the Michigan Avenue entrance, are by the Tiffany Company of New York. Two smaller examples in the vestibule were designed by the English pre-Raphaelite painter Edward Burne-Jones and executed by his great contemporary and countryman William Morris. The murals are by Frederic Clay Bartlett, a Chicago artist whose work also graces the Bartlett Gymnasium at the University of Chicago and the University Club of Chicago (8). (Bartlett was the donor of the distinguished Birch-Bartlett collection of paintings at the Art Institute of Chicago.) For many years the Second Presbyterian Church served a wealthy congregation that included residents of Prairie Avenue as well as Mrs. Abraham Lincoln and her son Robert Todd Lincoln.

126

McCormick Place   (1971, 1986)
South Lake Shore Drive and 23d Street
Architects: C. F. Murphy & Associates
    (1971); Skidmore, Owings & Merrill
    (1986)

This immense complex of exposition halls has had a tumultuous history as well as a steadily changing appearance due not solely to the constant and growing need for commercial exhibition space in a city traditionally known as a national convention center. The opening of McCormick Place in 1960 was accompanied by a chorus of complaints, never fully abated, about its siting on the edge of a lake front Chicagoans have long sought to keep free of impediments. The original building, by Shaw, Metz & Associates, is remembered as an uninspired piece of architecture de-

stroyed—mercifully, some would say—by fire in 1967. It was replaced in 1971 by a decidedly superior structure now known as McCormick Place East, whose massive trussed roof and recessed glass walls recall Mies van der Rohe's National Gallery in Berlin, an association traceable to the experience the chief designer, Gene Summers, had in Mies's office before he joined C. F. Murphy & Associates.

In 1986 the need for expanded space led to the construction of a second hall, by Skidmore, Owings & Merrill, known as McCormick Place North, across Lake Shore Drive to the west. This building, its roof supported by cables attached to two rows of six huge pylons each, also suggests a Miesian influence in the treatment of the surface of its four opaque polished metal facades, where a configuration of lines expressive of the interior roof trusses recalls Mies's unbuilt 1953 Convention Hall. Here the homage is less successful than in the 1971 building, mostly on account of indifferent proportioning and detailing, with the result that McCormick Place East and North bear little visual kinship with each other.

A third structure still in the planning stages with completion announced for 1997, is expected to be erected di-

rectly south of the north building. It is intended to contain more than 1,000,000 square feet of exhibition space, thus doubling the capacity of McCormick Place as a whole. The commissioned architects are Thompson, Ventulett, Stainback & Associates of Atlanta.

127

Illinois Institute of Technology Campus (1939–58)
South State Street, between 31st and 35th streets
Architect: Ludwig Mies van der Rohe; associated architects at different times: Holabird & Root; Friedman, Alschuler & Sincere; Pace Associates

A very long time was available to Mies to design this campus: he began the project in 1939 and finished the first main campus building in 1946 (after two research buildings

constructed during the war). In this period Mies completed a transition from a design process centered on expression of the plan to one concerned with the expression of structure. His American manner emerged only after long and profound reflection and formed the basis for the remainder of his career.

His buildings on the campus demonstrate four variations on this theme. The regular frame, tightly bound, enclosed with taut panels of brick and glass, predominates, as in Alumni, Perlstein, Wishnick, and Siegel halls. The concrete frames of the three apartment towers express these ideas in a high rise. The bearing-wall brick of the chapel encloses a focused, symmetrical, directional space unique on the campus. The unitary space created by the exoskeletal structure of S. R. Crown Hall is one of his most beautiful expressions of the pavilion temple.

The campus plan itself is an arrangement of form and space in which the buildings and the voids between them engage in a stately dialogue. Mies's elegant progressions provide a variety of experience unexpected in forms that seem at first so severe.

Following Mies's dismissal as campus architect in 1958, Skidmore, Owings & Merrill added several buildings, among them the library and student union, sited according to Mies's plan but otherwise unsuccessful. The single later building of distinction is Keating Hall (1966), designed by Myron Goldsmith of SOM.

128

St. Gabriel Church (1887)
4501 South Lowe
Architects: Burnham & Root

This building is remarkable in the bold massing of the
chief elements, including the chapels at the rear. The effect
of breadth and strength is emphasized by the subtle batter,
nicely worked out in the brick at the foot of the walls. The
tower has been lowered by the removal of a section that
was originally just below the present top story. The latter
has been rebuilt in line with the lower stories, whereas it
once projected beyond them. The tower has thus lost in
force as well as in height. The entrance porch has been
added, and there are minor changes in the buttresses. The
breadth and spaciousness of the original interior have been
maintained by the broad vaulted shapes of the ceiling, although there has been some remodeling, especially in the
northern part.

129

Kenwood District   CL

Between East 47th and East 51st streets,
   South Blackstone Avenue and South
   Drexel Boulevard

Kenwood developed as a comfortable suburb from 1856,
when Dr. John A. Kennicott built the first house there, to
1889, when the area was annexed to the City of Chicago.

Among the earliest surviving residences is the Italianate house at 4812 South Woodlawn, built, probably in the
1870s, when Kenwood was still sparsely settled. The Queen
Anne and Shingle styles appeared during the 1880s and the
following decade was marked by the revival of a number of
historical manners. Noteworthy examples include the Tudor revival house at 4815 South Woodlawn, designed by
Howard Van Doren Shaw and built in 1910; the Georgian
revival house at 4858 South Dorchester, designed by the
firm of Handy & Cady and built in 1897; and the Renaissance revival house at 4900 South Ellis, designed by Hora-

tio Wilson and Benjamin Marshall and built in 1899. The Magerstadt House, at 4930 South Greenwood Avenue, was designed by George W. Maher and built in 1906.

From the standpoint of architectural history, nothing in the district is more engaging than a pair of houses designed in 1892 by the twenty-five-year-old Frank Lloyd Wright. The George Blossom House at 4858 South Kenwood, while neo-Georgian on the exterior, contains several highly original interior spaces, and the Warren McArthur house immediately adjacent to it, at 4852 South Kenwood, is an eclectic amalgam of then-fashionable motifs. Both houses were done when Wright was working for the partnership of Dankmar Adler and Louis Sullivan, who expected him to devote his creative time exclusively to them. When it became apparent that he had been moonlighting on Kenwood Avenue and elsewhere, his tenure with the firm was terminated. The Blossom coach house, designed by Wright in 1907 and notable for its horizontal lines, illustrates his later, more mature stylistic approach.

Atrium Houses (1961)

1370 East Madison Park

Architect: Y. C. Wong

These reticent houses, designed by a student of Mies van der Rohe and modeled after that master's "courthouse" projects of the early 1930s, are closed up on the outside, opening to an interior court, or "atrium." The exterior brick walls are subdued and undecorated, with the headers at every sixth course making a scarcely noticeable variation. There is no cornice, only a simple beam at the top of the wall while a modest doorstep leads to the tall door openings.

Heller House (1897)   CL, NR
5132 South Woodlawn Avenue
Architect: Frank Lloyd Wright

Wright had not yet reached his full-blown Prairie style
when he executed this house. The arched windows of the
top story are vestiges of the nineteenth century and the
blocklike differentiation of the upper and lower portions
lacks the integration Wright later achieved. It is in the geometry of the row windows on the ground level that the
architect's more mature period is prefigured. The molded
plaster frieze at the top is by sculptor Richard Bock.

St. Thomas the Apostle (1922–24)   NR
5476 South Kimbark Avenue
Architect: Barry Byrne

The modernist manner of Byrne's design is worth noting in
view of the fact that this church was built at a time when
most American ecclesiastical architecture was consciously
and faithfully based on traditional forms. The concealed
steel beams that hold up the roof make possible the remarkable amplitude of the 95-by-193-foot worship space,
while the openness of that effect is underscored by the
sleek, abstracted patterns of the ceiling design and the
boldly original contours of the alcoves. That notwithstanding, a substantial quantity of terra-cotta ornament is
mounted along the cornice and around exterior surfaces of
windows and doorways, although it is of an exotic rather
than conventional order. The most arresting components of
the interior decorative program are the bronze bas-reliefs of
the Stations of the Cross, interpreted in the Art Deco mode
by the Italian-born American sculptor Alfeo Faggi.

University Building   (1937)
5551 South University Avenue
Architects: George F. and William Keck

This modestly scaled apartment building is one of the earliest examples in Chicago of the modern architecture associated with the International Style. As such it relies for its
effect on a clarity of composition and an abstracted rectilinear form, both precluding the ornament still commonly
practiced at the time by designers in the Art Deco mode.

Promontory Apartments (1949)
5530 South Shore Drive
Architects: Mies van der Rohe; Pace
   Associates; Holsman, Holsman &
   Klekamp

The first high-rise building erected by Mies after his 1938
emigration from Berlin to Chicago, Promontory is typical
of the post–World War II trend toward simple style, emphasis on structure, and care in planning, for both cost and
efficiency. Light-colored brick panels and aluminum window frames are set into a reinforced concrete frame that is
emphasized by the projection of the columns. Because of
the greater load on the lower stories, the columns are
stepped back on the exterior at the sixth, eleventh, and sixteenth stories; they are also scored every story to soften the
effect of the steps by integrating them with the overall design.

Museum of Science and Industry (1892)
South Lake Shore Drive at East 57th Street
Architects: Charles B. Atwood of D. H.
    Burnham & Co. (1892); Graham,
    Anderson, Probst & White (1929, 1933,
    1937, 1940); Shaw, Naess & Murphy (1937,
    1938); Hammell, Green & Abrahamson
    (1986).

Built as a temporary structure to house the Palace of Fine
Arts at the World's Columbian Exposition of 1893, this
building reflects the classical revival styles that prevailed at
the fair. The principal source is the nineteenth-century
Beaux-Arts ideal of a large, formal civic edifice, complex
but rigorously axial in its planning. The immense sprawl of
the building and its references to antique origins are the
most telling evidences of this. The portico and the wings
are expressed in a free treatment of the Ionic order. The
domes derive from Roman precedent and various details,
especially the caryatids and the metope reliefs, are taken respectively from the Erechtheion and the Parthenon, on the
Acropolis in Athens. (The chief architect Atwood, so con-
versant here with historical forms, would only a year later
complete the design of the Reliance Building [23], one of
the most technologically innovative structures of its day.)

   After the Columbian Exposition closed, this building
housed the collections of the Field Museum of Natural History until 1920, when a new Field Museum was completed
at the south end of Grant Park (14). Atwood's structure remained empty, deteriorating badly until the mid-1920s,
when Julius Rosenwald, president of Sears, Roebuck and
Co., proposed its rehabilitation as a museum of science and
technology. Inspired by the Deutsches Museum in Munich,
Rosenwald contributed a generous endowment to the creation of a similar institution in Chicago.

The reconstruction of the exterior of the museum, carried out in limestone, proceeded in several phases between 1929 and 1940, under the direction of Graham, Anderson, Probst & White. The interior was reconstituted, likewise progressively, in the late 1930s, by Shaw, Naess & Murphy. Most recently, in 1986, the Henry Crown Space Center, a domed structure enclosing the 350-seat Omnimax theater, was added along the museum's east elevation. The architects were Hammell, Green & Abrahamson of Minneapolis.

Constant changes over the years have kept the interior space far more modern in style than the exterior in its classicism, but in many places the evolving plan has been confounding to visitors. Recognizing this, the museum has commissioned Loebl, Schlossman & Hackl to assist in carrying out the design of "MSI 2000," a master plan intended to reorganize the interior into a simpler, more comprehensive pattern of thematic zones.

University of Chicago Campus (1891–)
Bounded by 57th and 59th Streets,
   University and Ellis avenues

This is one of the premier campus designs in the country,
in large part because a unified plan was conceived at the
very beginning and adhered to during the first four decades
of the university's growth.

Founded in 1891 with a substantial endowment from
John D. Rockefeller, the university early commissioned
Henry Ives Cobb to design the campus and its buildings.
Inspired by the example of the earliest English universities,
Cobb chose Gothic as the dominant style in Chicago and
Bedford limestone as his basic building material.

As conceived in the original plan and fully intact today, the quadrangles occupy the four-block area between
57th and 59th streets from University to Ellis Avenue. This
space, the heart of the campus, is bisected along the east-
west axis. To the north and south of that line, two pairs of

quadrangles are defined, each pair separated by a court that opens onto the central area. Later additions to the university are located on all sides of this original campus.

The main masses of the university are located on the north border of the broad Midway Plaisance, a concourse left over from the 1893 Columbian Exposition. The exterior of the quadrangle area is a long, nearly uninterrupted row of facades crowned by the twin towers of the old Harper Library.

A number of the early buildings of this composition were designed by Cobb himself. Cobb Hall (1891), the earliest, is one of these, although it was named for a benefactor, not for the designer. Also by Cobb are Ryerson Physical Laboratory (1894) and Kent Chemical Laboratory (1894). After the turn of the century, Shepley, Rutan & Coolidge became the campus architects. Designers from this Boston firm, successor to the office of H. H. Richardson, had already been responsible for the Art Institute of Chicago (13) and the Chicago Public Library (now the Chicago Cultural

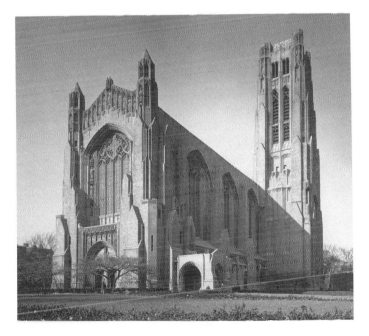

Center, 10). In following Cobb's plan at the university, they had largely defined the present configuration of the quadrangles by 1915. Their efforts included Bartlett Gymnasium and the old Law School, both completed in 1904. Thereafter, commissions were awarded to various independent architects for individual buildings throughout the campus, some of them worthy of note here. Rosenwald Hall (1915), an excellent study in the Gothic manner, was designed by Holabird & Roche, the most prolific architects of the Chicago school. Howard Van Doren Shaw, who frequently employed traditional forms in original ways, designed the Quadrangle Club, built in 1922. The intimate, richly decorated Bond Chapel, was built in 1926 by Coolidge & Hodgson. This firm, successor to Shepley, Rutan & Coolidge, did several other campus buildings during the 1920s.

The most monumental single edifice on the campus is Rockefeller Memorial Chapel (1928), a major example of the later American Gothic revival by one of its leading practitioners, Bertram G. Goodhue. Its massive solidity contrasts boldly with the lighter Gothic of the Fourth Presbyterian Church (75), by Goodhue's earlier partner Ralph A. Cram.

The interruption of building activity by the Depression and World War II had a major effect on American architecture as a whole and no less so on the later additions to the university. The traditional reliance on historical style gave way to modernist modes, with the result that recent campus buildings exhibit a variety of latter-day manners reflective of the individual designers who produced them.

The last recognizable effort in Gothic is the Administration Building of 1948, designed by Holabird, Root & Burgee, a structure with little to recommend it except a tolerable compatibility with its surroundings. Later commissions went to architects of clearly more contemporary style orientation. Eero Saarinen's Woodward Court residence hall was completed in 1958 and his Law School complex in 1960. The angled glass walls of the Law School Library dominate Saarinen's composition, which also includes a low-rise classroom wing and an auditorium structure in the shape of an eight-pointed star. Ludwig Mies van der Rohe

is represented by his Social Service Administration Building of 1965. One of the more respectable recent modernist works is the Kersten Physics Teaching Center by Holabird & Root, completed in 1985. Some observers have found the Gothic towers of the original buildings faintly echoed in I. W. Colburn's Henry Hinds Laboratory for the Geophysical Sciences of 1969 (done in collaboration with J. Lee Jones) and his Cummings Life Science Center of 1973 (in collaboration with Schmidt, Garden & Erickson and Harold H. Hellman, university architect). A comparably historical allusion has been cited in Skidmore, Owings & Merrill's Joseph Regenstein Library of 1970, in which Gothic verticality seems subtly echoed in the vertical bands of limestone and narrow slotlike windows of the facade.

The Cochrane-Woods Fine Arts Center and Smart Museum of Art (1974), by Edward Larrabee Barnes, is a piece of geometric modernism indebted more to the International Style than to any memory of a Gothic past. It is, in fact, closer in both character and location to the Court Theater just to the west of it, designed by Harry Weese in 1981. The Smart Museum houses most of the university's art collection, with the notable exception of the outstanding trove of ancient near eastern art at the Oriental Institute (1931), by Mayers, Murray & Phillips, successors to the Goodhue office.

137

Robie House (1910)   CL, NR
5757 South Woodlawn Avenue
Architect: Frank Lloyd Wright

The Robie House, completed at the end of the decade in
which Wright explored and perfected the Prairie style, is
one of the most famous private residences in the world and
by consensus among the most brilliant designs in the history of American architecture. Adapted to a narrow city
lot, it nonetheless achieves an amplitude of form enlivened
by a powerful, tightly organized interpenetration of masses.
The long limestone sills, the broad overhanging roofs, even
the slender "Roman bricks," contribute to the horizontality
said by Wright to reflect the midwestern prairie—hence
the name standardly applied to the style. Interior space
flows freely between living and dining room around the
great hearth. Illumination is provided by rows of rich, geo-
metrical leaded glass windows and by a series of inventively
conceived globular lamps.

The house is occupied by the University of Chicago's Office of Alumni Affairs. The original dining room furniture is part of the collection of the university's Smart Museum.

South Shore Country Club (1916)   NR
South Shore Drive and East 71st Street
Architects: Marshall & Fox

Incorporated in 1906 as a suburban club in an area then
largely undeveloped, South Shore Country Club grew and
prospered as a residential community developed around it
in the early years of this century. Membership dwindled as
the community changed in the 1960s and in 1974 the club
was sold to the Chicago Park District. The original club-
house of 1906, modeled after one in Mexico City, was
moved closer to the lake when the present structure went
up in 1916, and was demolished in 1975. The present club-
house shows a complex silhouette with towers, wings, and
projecting colonnades. The facades are rather plain, and the
walls are covered with cement stucco reminiscent of Medi-
terranean architecture. The broad roofs are shingled with
clay tiles. On the ground floor tall windows reflect the
grand spaces within, providing those spaces with a com-

manding view of the lake and the club grounds. Restoration of the buildings, begun in 1978, is ongoing. Much of the exterior work is by the Chicago Park District Design Services while interior spaces were renovated by Norman DeHaan.

139

South Pullman District   (1880–94)   CL, NR
South Cottage Grove Avenue to South
    Langley Street between East 111th and
    East 115th streets
Architects: Solon S. Beman, Nathan F.
    Barrett

The town of Pullman was built by the Pullman Company to accommodate its manufacturing activities and provide housing for its employees; as such it was America's first completely planned company town

The site consisted of roughly 4000 acres of land along the western shore of Lake Calumet close by the Illinois Central Railroad tracks. All the buildings were designed by Beman and the public spaces were laid out by Barrett, a landscape architect. Much of the original complex has been demolished or subject to depredation, including the 195-foot water tower that once dominated the town, as well as the great interior spaces of the Arcade, a multipurpose structure that housed stores, a bank, a post office, a library, and a theater. Even so, the shape and substance of the community are still largely perceptible. The charming Florence Hotel, with its profusion of roofs, dormers and gables reflective of the Queen Anne style, stands across the public park from the Greenstone Church, a crisp little variation on the Romanesque. The side streets are lined with row residences, originally more than 1400 of them, mostly single family units. A remarkable number of them, ranging from humble to elegant, have been preserved.

If Chicago's reputation for loyalties to its professional sports franchises is exceptional among its sister cities, so is the age of the facilities in which the reputation has been forged. Until old Comiskey Park was demolished and replaced by its namesake in 1991, the newest of the city's four major

arenas, the Chicago Stadium, was more than sixty years old. Chicagoan Zachary Taylor Davis is remembered for little more than his designs of old Comiskey Park (1910) and Wrigley Field, but those two steel-framed, brick-enclosed structures were legendary for their fitness as ball parks in which the spectators were optimally close to the action. Wrigley Field still exists, its nickname—"the friendly confines"—deriving largely from its ivy-covered walls and ancient, hand-operated but uncommonly informative scoreboard. Soldier Field, so called in memory of Americans killed in World War I, was designed for a capacity of 55,000, but adaptations have been made to accommodate larger crowds, such as the more than 100,000 who viewed the celebrated Jack Dempsey–Gene Tunney heavyweight championship prize fight of 1927. Reflecting the neo-classical architecture of its neighbors, the Field Museum and the Shedd Aquarium, it is notable for the Doric columns that rise from the tops of the two long sides of its grandstands.

Demolished 1995

More recently, the competition for leisure dollars has led some owners of sports franchises in Chicago to destroy their historic homes and build new facilities. Both Comiskey Park (White Sox) and the Chicago Stadium (Blackhawks and Bulls) have been replaced by new facilities, on sites adjacent to their predecessors. In both cases the conclusion of the new denizens of these facilities is that while it is easier to get and recycle a beer, in other ways the new facilities are exactly the soulless corporate hulks that were feared.

The Suburbs

By now it is common knowledge that urban demographic pressure has moved from the city to the suburbs, with the chief agency of the shift almost universally acknowledged as the automobile. Since World War II the population of Chicago has declined as surely as that of the surrounding metropolitan area has grown. Nothing stimulated this realignment more than the increased availability of motorized transportation to citizens whose ability to move about relatively freely and rapidly has quickened the exodus from the crowded precincts of the old city to what is commonly perceived as the more open and attractive newer towns.

Structures expressive of the shift have appeared, most obviously the superhighway and the shopping mall, neither of them thinkable without the latter-day private motor car. Moreover, while the industrial parks, office complexes and corporate headquarters, planned communities and tract developments of the postwar years have more demonstrable historical precedent, many of them are just as surely the spawn of the automobile.

History also offers the reminder, however, that the phenomenon of swift exurban expansion is hardly as recent as it might appear at first. Chicago has spread outward from its ancient downtown center in proportion to the evolution of transportation facilities. By the 1850s, less than two decades after the formal incorporation of Chicago, a single horse-drawn omnibus rolling on planked streets could carry a dozen or more people as far north as Lincoln Park. A few years later similarly powered vehicles, moving twice as fast as a man could walk, operated on rails. Cable cars followed, and electric trains. By the time of the Chicago Fire, railroad lines not only connected the central business district to such independent towns—thus "suburbs"—as Evanston, Hinsdale, Washington Heights, and Hyde Park, but enabled the inhabitants of those erstwhile far-flung places to work in the city. The railroad was the great instrument of suburban growth in Chicago and other older American metropolises well before the auto counted for much. Rails radiated outward from downtown, and along the lines they traced the communities took form. Chicago was able to incorporate many of these (Hyde Park and Washington Heights among them), but after 1893 the city limits changed only a little, while existent suburbs grew and new ones were created.

The burgeoning of the city's outer metropolitan area between 1870 and 1940 was significant enough to produce an architecture as important as it was various. Probably the most celebrated example of this is the body of revolutionary residential work of Frank Lloyd Wright and his followers, the so-called Prairie school, that left its legacy most prominently in Oak Park, River Forest, and Riverside, but the more conservative house designs of David Adler and Howard Van Doren Shaw, principally in Lake Forest, warrant attention in their own right.

Other architectural classifications are similarly worthy of note. Achievements in urban planning by Almerin Hotchkiss in laying out the plat of Lake Forest, by Frederick Law Olmsted in doing the same for Riverside, and by Solon S. Beman in designing virtually all the buildings of Pullman have earned those communities a lasting place in the textbooks. Less publicized but comparable in quality as military architecture are the buildings and grounds of Fort Sheridan, most of them by the firm of Holabird & Roche. Some arresting ecclesiastical architecture was also put up in Chicago suburbs

during the first half of the century, none more spectacular than Louis Bourgeois's Baha'i House of Worship in
Wilmette. The campus of Northwestern University in
Evanston is the most important collective example of
suburban architecture in the service of education, while
Crow Island School in Winnetka by Eliel and Eero
Saarinen, Perkins, Wheeler & Will has the distinction of
representing a union of progressive educational philoso-
phy and, for its time, progressive architectural form.
Moreover, well before World War II the suburbs had become sufficiently like the city in their activities and functions that their accomplishments in commercial and
industrial buildings are not unworthy of the company of
their more renowned city relatives. In this category the
spectrum extends from the patrician Lake Forest shopping center, Market Square, to the vernacular manner
and monumental scale of the Western Electric Factory in
Cicero.

Thus the impact of the automobile was decisive
only after World War II. Significantly, while the population of the city had continued to rise prior thereto, if at
a slower rate than that of the suburbs, it began to fall in
the 1950s. An assortment of reasons can be cited for this,
but the motor car accelerated the process uniquely, and
from an architectural point of view left a landscape
markedly different from any preceding it. The multilane
roads that became known as expressways, visually striking examples of modern construction techniques especially at their points of intersection, altered the whole
metropolitan matrix, while giving rise in the suburbs to
commercial complexes strung along them in intervals
too vast to be comprehended as communal in any traditional sense. At the same time and like a wind of great
force and multiple directions, the decentralization
caused by the automobile has produced eddies and
swirls, new forms of congealment like the Old Orchard,

Oak Brook, and Woodfield shopping malls, new towns like Elk Grove Village and Hoffman Estates, industrial administrative complexes like Baxter Laboratories and Ameritech, even the "tract mansion" developments that have most recently mushroomed around the edges of the established suburbs. The material success of many of these new enterprises has emptied out not only much of Chicago but the centers of some of the older villages too. The pace of change in the last years of the century only quickens.

While the ultimate value of automobilia to society at large continues to be debated, any architectural study of Chicago or other American cities (increasingly those in Europe as well) must make a place for it alongside the more conventional building forms that have also gone up during the last several generations throughout a metropolitan area that has not died, as the many doom-sayers of the 1970s and 1980s predicted for the cities of the national northeast quadrant, but stayed remarkably, if sometimes troublesomely, alive.

MAP 9 NORTHERN SUBURBS

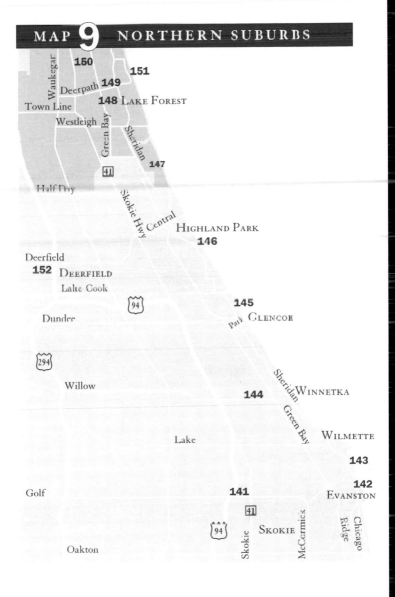

Waukegan
150
151
Deerpath **149**
Town Line **148** LAKE FOREST
Westleigh
Green Bay
Sheridan
147
41
Half Day
Skokie Hwy
Central
HIGHLAND PARK
146
Deerfield
152 DEERFIELD
Lake Cook
94
Dundee
145
Park GLENCOE
294
Willow
Sheridan
Green Bay
WINNETKA
144
Lake
WILMETTE
143
142
EVANSTON
Golf
141
41
94
Skokie
SKOKIE
McCormick
Chicago Ridge
Oakton

THE SUBURBS

MAP 10 WESTERN SUBURBS

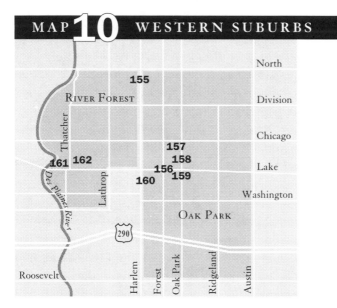

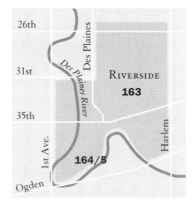

Old Orchard Shopping Center (1957)
Golf Road and Skokie Highway, Skokie
Architects: Loebl, Schlossman & Bennett

Perhaps more than any other product of contemporary popular culture, the shopping mall symbolizes the enormous growth of American suburbs since World War II and the impact of the device that generated the growth, the automobile.

The motor car has enabled whole populations not only to live and work well beyond the limits of the city, but to trade there as well, in wholly planned concentrations of retail outlets—the malls. Since they are usually built just far enough from population centers to be reached easily by auto, they have made main streets largely obsolete.

The most modest example of the new genre is the strip mall, where low storefronts are lined up in a long row behind vast parking lots. In the high-budget malls, on the other hand (e.g., Woodfield, 154), the shops face inward to roofed corridors that run the length and width of what amounts to an introverted structure.

Old Orchard is a cross between the two types or, in another sense, neither of them. It is bordered by a parking area typical of malls, but its shops are organized in groups rather than a single building, with the spaces between them given over to connecting pathways. Thus pedestrian traffic moves both indoors and outdoors. Judicious landscaping enhances buildings of respectably consistent design that have kept their age fairly well. Old Orchard has proven one of the most durable shopping centers in the Chicago area.

142

Northwestern University Campus (1851–)
Sheridan Road between Clark and Lincoln
    streets, Evanston

Founded in 1851, Northwestern University did not initially have a master plan for the design of its Evanston campus. Prairie school architect George Maher prepared such a plan in 1908, but the university never adopted its formal, axial pattern. Consequently, the buildings are rather randomly sited along the 4,000-foot stretch of lakeshore campus. The university's first building was constructed in 1855. Now demolished, it was a Greek revival frame structure designed by John Mills Van Osdel, Chicago's earliest architect of note. The oldest campus building standing today is the 1869 University Hall, designed in a somewhat naive Gothic style. During the last thirty years of the nineteenth century, a number of undistinguished, and largely unrelated, revivalist buildings were added. At the end of the first decade of this century, George Maher designed two campus buildings, in addition to his campus plan: Patten Gymnasium of 1909

(demolished 1940), with a powerful vaulted structure whose arched facade directly expressed the interior space, and Swift Hall, also of 1909, representative of the best tradition of small Chicago school commercial structures.

One of the most prominent buildings on campus, by virtue of its location at the far side of a broad, open meadow, is the Deering Library of 1932. Designed by James

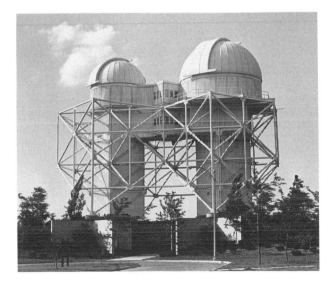

Gamble Rogers, it is an example of the collegiate Gothic style popular for university campuses during the early twentieth century. Its superb siting was disturbed in the early 1970s by the construction of Loebl, Schlossman, Bennett & Dart's Leverone Hall and School of Education, which interrupt the expanse of Deering Meadow and break the crescent configuration of the older buildings facing the meadow.

In 1961, the university decided to expand its campus to the east by building on landfill. Sixty-five additional acres were created between 1962 and 1964. In 1966, Lindheimer Astronomical Observatory was built at the northeast corner of the landfill. Designed by Skidmore, Owings & Merrill, this abstractly sculptural composition consists of two domed observation towers clad in sheet metal and joined by a bridge near the top. A trussed framework of steel tubing braces, supports, and unites the towers. The Core and Research Library of 1969 was also designed by Skidmore, Owings & Merrill. The three pavilions of reinforced concrete are connected at the base to each other and to the Deering Library. The configuration of the pavilions reflects the radial arrangement of the stacks and study carrels inside. The supporting concrete columns, projecting limestone panels, and narrow, vertical bands of windows create a vertical rhythm that animates the exterior.

Recent additions to the southeast corner of the campus, most of them devoted to the arts, include—ironically— some of the least artful architecture the university has ever put up. The Barbara and Garry Marshall Studio wing, John J. Louis Hall, the Marjorie Ward Marshall Dance Center, the Josephine Louis Theatre and the Mary and Leigh Block Gallery are housed in structures that individually and together resemble ill-proportioned heaps of whitewashed packing boxes.

143

Baha'i House of Worship (1953) NR
Sheridan Road at Linden Avenue, Wilmette
Architect: Louis Bourgeois

Rising 191 feet from the ground floor to its pinnacle, the
temple contains four stories of lace-like reinforced concrete,
with tall windows and elaborate carvings. Although construction began in 1920, work was not completed until
1953. The necessary funds, totaling $3 million, were raised
solely by temple members as their gift to the peoples of the
world.

The building has nine sides, each with an entrance
door. Carved into the stone above the entrances, likewise above each of the nine alcoves, is a quotation from
Bah'u'llah, founder of the Baha'i faith. For the Baha'is the

number nine, the largest single number, is a symbol of unity and oneness.

The simplicity of the Baha'i religion is reflected inside the temple. Rows of chairs fill the large auditorium, and only drapes hang from the walls—there are no altars, no images, no candles. From any seat one can view Lake Michigan, the gardens, or the quiet houses on Linden Avenue.

144

Crow Island School (1940)

1112 Willow, Winnetka
Architects: Eliel and Eero Saarinen;
   Perkins, Wheeler & Will

This building, situated in a spacious and leafy suburban setting, was one of the first to revive a modern scholastic

architecture that owed so much to the efforts of Dwight Perkins in Chicago in 1905–10. The local board of education wanted a school that would fit the emotional and intellectual needs of children as well as their physical scale. The aim was to make the school environment as pleasant and comfortable as possible, so that it might become a positive tool in enhancing the learning process. The architects began with the design of a single classroom, a self-contained prototype that might be used with suitable variations for all age groups. The ultimate design then became a matter of multiplying these units along three wings extending from a central section devoted to common facilities. The class rooms project outward in subsidiary wings from the corridors, each pair of rooms enclosing its associated outdoor play space. The warm color and pleasant texture of brick and wood, the glazed ceramic sculpture set at intervals in the exterior walls, and the delightful scale enliven the design.

145

North Shore Congregation Israel   (1963, 1983)

1185 Sheridan Road, Glencoe

Architects: Minoru Yamasaki (1963);
  Hammond, Beeby & Babka (1983)

Erected twenty years apart, the two major buildings of the complex are a large and a small sanctuary, each with adjoining areas serving a variety of functions.

The Yamasaki temple of 1963 is especially noteworthy for its unique interior structural system. Each of the component forms of the space combines column and roof slab in a single continuous element of reinforced concrete rising from a thin stemlike form at the base and opening gradually into a broad leaflike cantilever at the top. The two rows of these cantilevers, one on each side of the central longitudinal axis, constitute the roof of the tabernacle. The space between any pair of "stems" is filled with a thin flat slab of concrete bordered by amber glass. On the exterior,

each end of the tabernacle is closed by still another leaflike form—in this case a broad slab with a central rib from which two sets of veins curve outward and downward.

If the Yamasaki sanctuary is an example of that architect's idiosyncratic late modern style, the addition by Hammond, Beeby & Babka conforms to the post-modernist tastes prevalent during the early 1980s. From the outside, its principal mass is a cleanly simplified brick cylinder to which a portico based on a classical Palladian motif has been added. The main interior space, the Perlman Sanctuary, is effectively a cylinder within a cylinder that recalls the box-within-a-box concept that Frank Lloyd Wright expressed in his Unity Temple in Oak Park (159). The decor of the Perlman Sanctuary abounds in classical features like round arches, oculi, and Tuscan Doric columns. A central axis leads to the Ark. Built to fill the congregation's need for a worship area smaller than the Yamasaki temple, the sanctuary leads through an east exit to the Rebecca B. Crown Social Hall, an ample rectangular room from which a handsome view of Lake Michigan may be enjoyed.

146

Willits House   (1902)
1445 Sheridan Road, Highland Park
Architect: Frank Lloyd Wright

One of the earliest and most successful examples of Wright's Prairie style residences, this house occupies its Sheridan Road site with a majestic sweep outward from its core. The influence of Japanese domestic architecture is evident in the central tract, its stucco surfaces activated by wood strips and dominated by wide overhanging eaves. The interior is a definitive realization of Wright's concept of an open, flowing space that reduces much of the sense of the rooms as enclosed cubicles. A huge fireplace is the physical and spiritual center of the cruciform plan. The major spaces—entry, living room, and dining room—that extend out from the hearth are lit by leaded glass windows on three sides. Sleeping rooms on the second floor are similarly grouped around the core. A gardener's cottage on the same site, also by Wright, has been remodeled as a separate residence.

147

Fort Sheridan Historical District (1888–1891)

Main Entrance: Sheridan Road, between
  Highwood to the south and Lake Forest
  to the north
Architects: Holabird & Roche; Ossian
  Simonds

Isolated voluntarily by its military mission and involuntarily by the consciously exclusive society of its elegant neighbors Lake Forest and Highland Park, Fort Sheridan has been one of the best-kept architectural secrets of the North

Shore. Yet in the unity of its building styles, its planning and its distribution of functions, it qualifies as one of the most successful urbanistic accomplishments in the Chicago metropolitan area.

The main entrance leads on an east-west axis to a large parade ground, designed by Ossian Simonds, that serves equally as a mall. Its dominant feature is a lofty and dignified formal watchtower, the most imposing of the many buildings erected by Holabird & Roche in the fort's historical district. The common yellow brick used throughout the post lends a plain but impressive consistency to the styles—chiefly Queen Anne, neo-Romanesque, and vernacular variations—of the administrative buildings, depots, shops, drill buildings and housing units. Especially noteworthy are the three looping lanes of officers' houses radiating from the mall eastward toward the lake. Embellished by handsome stands of oaks and maples and separated by

generous expanses of lawn, the houses are mostly gabled prisms with arched porches and occasional turret corners.

Fort Sheridan, one of the many military and naval facilities to be discontinued by the Federal government as part of a massive budgetary cutback, is scheduled to be turned into a reserve support center in 1993. The fate of its buildings and grounds has been debated at length and has not yet been resolved.

148

Lake Forest

Although settled as early as the 1830s, Lake Forest did not begin to take on the character of a community until after wealthy Chicago Presbyterians elected in the 1850s to establish an institution of higher learning there. Financial reverses delayed the founding of the school later known as Lake Forest University and finally as Lake Forest College, but by the 1870s the village was widely accepted throughout the Chicago area as the most socially prestigious of the city's suburbs.

The first notable architectural achievement was the town plan of 1857, now attributed to Almerin Hotchkiss, a surveyor and planner associated with St. Louis. An informal network of curving roads echoing and sometimes following the contours of the ravines that wind down to the lake, the plat is an outgrowth of the romantic tradition and traceable to eighteenth-century English gardens, early nineteenth-century American communal cemeteries and parks, and the theories of naturalistic landscaping promoted in America by Andrew Jackson Downing. Hotchkiss's plan preceded Frederick Law Olmsted's more celebrated layout of Riverside (163) by at least a decade. It also encouraged the early rurality of Lake Forest as well as the town's reputation for leisurely, untrammeled society.

The opening of the Onwentsia Country Club in 1893 was instrumental in prompting members of Chicago's most famous families, including the McCormicks, the Swifts, and the Armours, to build homes in an increasingly urbane Lake Forest. Slowly the custom of summer residence there

gave way to year-round living. Thus the town's business center, Market Square, as well as its numerous grand mansions, were built after the turn of the century.

The show of wealth traditionally associated with Lake Forest society is still strikingly evident, most prominently in the estates along Lake Road and Green Bay Road, more than a few of which were designed by Howard Van Doren Shaw and David Adler.

149

Market Square (1916)
700 North Western Avenue, Lake Forest
Architect: Howard Van Doren Shaw

Certifiably one of the oldest planned shopping centers in the nation, Market Square is a charming congeries of traditional styles, its gabled, Tudor half-timbered row houses (with shops downstairs) in easy accord with the classicism of the Marshall Field's store and the Northern European eclecticism of the two towers flanking the entrance to the area. The detailing in several of the buildings reflects Shaw's personal devotion to the international Arts and Crafts movement.

Ragdale (1894)
1240 North Green Bay Road, Lake Forest
Architect: Howard Van Doren Shaw

Shaw designed more than thirty private homes in Lake
Forest, several of them more imposing but none more in-
gratiating than his own residence. Ragdale's indebtedness to
the Art and Crafts movement is apparent both inside and
out. The white stucco surfaces of the house are appropriate
to its modest dimensions. The front facade, crowned by a
pair of gables, features windows with flower boxes and a
vine-covered loggia. The choice interior space is the dining
room, visible from the entry hall through two window
screens studded with diamond-shaped panes. The Ragdale
estate as a whole is notable on several accounts. One of the
outbuildings is a remodeled barn dating from the 1840s,
faintly Greek revival in profile, the oldest standing structure in Lake Forest. Sixteen acres of land sloping gently to
the west include stretches of virgin prairie. Now owned by
the city of Lake Forest, the property is the home of the
Ragdale Foundation, the most important artists' colony in
the midwest.

Mrs. Kersey Coates Reed House (1930)
1315 Lake Road, Lake Forest
Architect: David Adler

One of the great American society architects of the twentieth century, David Adler left several of his most distinguished works in Lake Forest. He was an eclectic by habit, drawing almost omnivorously on a wide variety of historical manners and combining them in happy stylistic marriages. The Reed House owes something to the plans of Palladian villas in its main tract with symmetrically extending arms, while the Georgian facade is clad in gray Pennsylvania mica stone. The interior is notable for a dramatic entry gallery that ends in an elegant curving staircase adorned in spare classical motifs. A mirrored powder room and a leather-lined library are among the other arresting features.

152

Baxter International (1975)
One Baxter Parkway
Deerfield
Architects: Skidmore, Owings & Merrill

The steady recent expansion, indeed the urbanization, of the Chicago suburban network has led more than a few major industries to move their plants and headquarters to sites outside the city. Among the most architecturally noteworthy is the Baxter Laboratories group near Deerfield, seen most readily and comprehensively from the Tri-State Tollway. Four steel-framed pavilions surround the Central Facilities Building that is the dominant element in the complex not only in size and structural inventiveness but in overall visual impact. It is crowned by a roof hung on cables suspended in turn from two powerful columns resting on caissons and rising 35 feet above roof level. More cables on the underside of the roof, fixed to the columns and extending upward from them, help to stiffen the roof.

The upper system is visible from the outside, while the lower is equally apparent from within the great cafeteria space that takes up most of the upper level. (The lower level is given over to a training school, an auditorium, a reception area, and an executive dining room.) The facade of the building is a massive wall of glass 288 feet long, 48 feet high and clad in white-painted aluminum.

273

153

Ameritech (1991)
2000 Ameritech Center Drive
    Hoffman Estates, Illinois
    Architects: Lohan Associates

During the last generation corporate headquarters have
been among the more common major architectural additions to the exurban landscape. When functioning, as they
often do, as the main tenants of large speculative office
buildings scattered along arterial roads and expressways,
they rarely add any sense of community to their environments. The best of them, contrarily, have tended simply to
isolate themselves more fully on large tracts of land, where
they amount to self-contained mini-cities with training, recreational, dining, and parking facilities attached to the offices in which the corporation's work is carried out.
Ameritech is one of the most ambitious of the latter type in
the Chicago area. Its faintly post-modernist decor is combined with the more structurally modernist treatment of
the arms extending outward from it, which enclose two
atriums at opposite ends of the building.

Woodfield Shopping Center (1971)
5 Woodfield Shopping Center, Golf Road
   and Route 53
Schaumburg
Architects: Jickling & Lyman

There seems no predictable end in sight to the spread of suburban shopping malls and the gargantuan business districts with which they are symbiotically connected. When Woodfield opened in 1971, it was billed as the largest indoor mall in the world, a superlative it has long since lost to more than a few global rivals. Even so, it remains huge enough that its dimensions cannot be taken in visually by its patrons, who indeed can scarcely make their way to its entrance except by automobile. Its exterior can be perceived in full only from the air, while internally the axes of its four arms are intentionally set ajog as they meet in the immense central court, thus insuring that no vista is too long to discourage a pedestrian shopper from traversing its full length. Four enormous sculptures are set at the far ends of the wings. Each of them is abstract; none is identified by title or artist. Despite this and other signs of anonymity, not

155

Oak Park and River Forest

Little in either natural topography or formal organization
differentiates the plans of Oak Park and its neighbor River
Forest from that of Chicago. Both suburbs are laid out on
the grid that is standard throughout the American middle
west as a whole and Chicago specifically. Indeed the opposite of Oak Park and River Forest within the greater metropolitan area must be Lake Forest and Riverside, each of
which was conceived by an identifiable individual as an informal web of picturesquely winding roads, moreover as a
perceptibly delimited community. Thus Oak Park and
River Forest, effectively extensions of the Chicago street
pattern, are more nearly suburbs in the exact sense of the
word, while Lake Forest and Riverside in their contain-
ment may be more properly regarded as exurban creations.

At the same time, since many of the towns at the edge
of Chicago are constructed on plans akin to those of Oak
Park and River Forest, there must be another reason for as-
signing the latter municipalities, particularly Oak Park, a
special place in the annals of Chicago architecture. His
name is Frank Lloyd Wright. A resident of Oak Park from
1889 to 1909, Wright not only left a rich legacy of buildings
there but attracted a coterie of followers who made up
what is commonly called the Prairie school.

More important, Wright drew from the tableland west
of Chicago the inspiration to produce a uniquely American
residential architecture. In the outward reach of its hori-

zontally expressed exterior forms and the openness of its interior plans, it was reflective of the seemingly endless and multidirectional expansion of the prairie. No understanding of Wright and his singular contribution to international architecture can be complete without an awareness of the dozens of houses he and his disciples left in Oak Park and River Forest.

156

Forest Avenue
Between Chicago Avenue and Ontario
Street, Oak Park

Oak Park is internationally renowned, mostly because of
the imprint left there by Frank Lloyd Wright and his followers of the Prairie school. (Among the latter, George W.
Maher, Thomas Eddy Tallmadge, John S. Van Bergen, and
Vernon Spencer Watson executed buildings in Oak Park.)

Wright's work in Oak Park is most concentrated along
the tree-lined stretch of Forest Avenue that runs from Chicago Avenue south to Ontario Street. Seven of the houses
on the street are by him, although most visitors make it a
point to pass by an eighth example, the house of Mrs.
Thomas H. Gale at 6 Elizabeth Court, a cul-de-sac that
jogs off Forest about halfway along this route. Wright's earliest expressive manner is the Shingle style treatment of his
own home (1889; 157), while one of the most mature
achievements in the Prairie manner is the Gale House
(1909; 158), the hard geometries of which prefigure European modernism of the 1920s.

Stylistically speaking, these two houses bracket a wide
array of types. The William H. Copeland House (at 400),
put up by another builder in 1873, was remodeled in 1908–
9 by Wright, who added his most typical touches to the in-

terior spaces. The Edward R. Hills House (at 313), dating
from 1874, is also a remodeled work (in 1906), but Wright's
hand was exercised far more thoroughly throughout, even
though the sloping roof lines are, for him, curiously retar-
dataire. The gables that dominate the Peter A. Beachy
House (at 238 [1906]) and Nathan G. Moore House (at 333
[1895, reconstructed by Wright in 1923 after a fire]) are
similarly uncharacteristic; indeed the openly derivative English Tudor features of the Moore House testify to Wright's
occasional willingness to accommodate himself to a client's
tastes. On the other hand, in the low, wide eaves and ribbon

casements of the Arthur Heurtley House (at 318 [1902])
and the all-stucco facade of the Frank W. Thomas House
(at 210 [1901]), Wright was clearly his own man, in com-
mand of the principles and devices that marked the fully
articulated Prairie style.

157

Frank Lloyd Wright Home and   NR
Studio (1889–98)
951 Chicago Avenue, Oak Park
Architect: Frank Lloyd Wright

Frank Lloyd Wright's house and studio, the construction of
which began in 1889 (when Wright was only twenty-two)
and continued for nearly a decade, provide a fascinating insight into the architect's process of maturation. The house,
facing Forest Avenue, was the first element to be built and
is derivative of the Shingle style of the 1880s. At the time
Wright was still employed by the firm of Adler & Sullivan
and had not as yet developed his own personal manner. It is
thus interesting to note that he used several pieces of the
ornamental castings from Adler & Sullivan's Auditorium

Building, which was under construction at the same time, in the ceiling of his living room.

The studio was built after Wright had established his own practice, and although connected to the house, it is a separate entity. The design anticipates Wright's work in the years after the turn of the century. The plan is a precursor of the open plans of later years.

In 1974, the National Trust for Historic Preservation acquired the house and entered into an agreement with the Frank Lloyd Wright Home and Studio Foundation, whereby the foundation was made responsible for operating the house and restoring it to its appearance in 1909, the last year Wright lived there. The restoration was completed in 1987.

Mrs. Thomas H. Gale House (1909) NR
6 Elizabeth Court, Oak Park
Architect: Frank Lloyd Wright

The house Frank Lloyd Wright designed for Mrs. Thomas
H. Gale in 1909 remains one of his most impressive essays
in small house design. The cantilevers, interlocking forms,
and voids—each tied to the central fireplace core—all combine to demonstrate the ability of Wright to integrate
simple shapes into a complex but lucidly functioning whole.
Some authorities have seen it as anticipating the spirit and
character of the International Style that was to develop, initially in Europe, later in America, over the next three decades.

This house can be favorably compared to any other of
Wright's works, although most often considered as a prefi-
guration to Fallingwater, built a quarter of a century later.

© Bill Crofton

Unitarian Universalist Church and Parish House (Unity Temple) (1906)

Lake Street at Kenilworth Avenue, Oak
  Park
Architect: Frank Lloyd Wright

This bold essay in concrete was Wright's solution to a problem presented by the modest budget of the small Unitarian congregation of Oak Park. Earlier he had employed concrete in the E-Z Polish Factory in Chicago, although he had suggested its use as early as 1894 in a design he called a "Concrete Monolithic Bank."

Unity Temple is actually two spaces, Unity Church and a parish house, connected by a low passage that contains the entrance. Both principal elements are lighted by clerestory windows and skylights featuring some of Wright's finest abstract glass designs. The auditorium is a cube with the pulpit projected well into the space, thus enhancing a sense of closeness between the speaker and the parishioners.

Two staircases at the rear of the hall lead to a three-sided balcony that offers a similar intimacy at the upper level. The stairwells are expressed externally by massive blocklike posts at all four corners of the building.

The parish house is a smaller cube with wings extending from two sides to provide classrooms and meeting spaces.

The ornamental concrete work of the exterior piers was repeated on each facade by reusing wooden molds for all six major walls.

At the initiative of the Unity Temple Restoration Foundation, a program of refurbishing has been pursued for over two decades. Work on the lay lights and the skylights of the auditorium is now complete. Plans are ongoing for the restoration of the cantilevered eaves in the auditorium. The color scheme has been returned to its original state.

160

Pleasant Home   (1899)
(John Farson House)
217 Home Avenue, Oak Park
Architect: George Washington Maher

This ambitious design by Maher declares his allegiance to the ideas of broadness of conception and simplification of mass and surface encouraged by Richardson at the Glessner

House (1887; 123) and accomplished by Wright in the
Winslow House (1893; 161). The stolid horizontality of the
house, with chiselled openings and smooth surfaces, and
the expanse of the parklike site declare this a house of great
presence and assurance. The broadness of the exterior is
continued on the interior, enriched and enlivened by the
use of exotic wood, tile work, art glass and metal. Since it is
now owned by the Village of Oak Park, plans have been
made to develop the building as a house museum. The collections of the Historical Society of Oak Park and River
Forest are also displayed in the building.

161

Winslow House (1894)   NR
515 Auvergne Place, River Forest
Architect: Frank Lloyd Wright

The William H. Winslow house, Frank Lloyd Wright's first
independent commission, is highly reminiscent of the work
of Louis Sullivan, particularly in the exterior, second-story
frieze and the fenestration. The planning is for Wright extremely formal, reflecting the relatively conservative attitude of the young architect at the time. Even so, the later
stable, or garage, at the rear of the house is freer in planning and demonstrates Wright's more mature style.

Drummond House (1909)   NR
559 Edgewood, River Forest
Architect: William Drummond

William Drummond, practicing both alone and with his partner, Louis Guenzel, was one of the most successful of the many persons trained by Frank Lloyd Wright in his Oak Park studio. In refining Wright's concept of the economical Prairie house in the design of his own house, he achieved an architectural gem. In fact, it stands immediately south of one of Wright's more admired works, the Isabel Roberts House of 1908.

The plan of the first floor of the Drummond House is almost completely open with only the kitchen separated. The second floor is done in a conventional manner. Throughout, the house is furnished with pieces designed by Drummond, which contribute to the effect of livability.

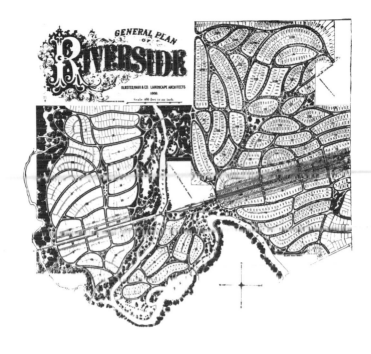

163

Riverside (1869)
Planner: Frederick Law Olmsted

Enough remains of the original plan and the early buildings of Riverside to keep intact the community's long-
standing reputation as one of the handsomest suburbs in
the Chicago area. The plat dates from 1869, when Frederick Law Olmsted, the most illustrious American landscape
architect of his day, laid out Riverside in a pattern of curving streets disposed on both sides of the parkland bordering
the Des Plaines River. Inspired by the romantic and to a
degree "anti-modern" belief in a townscape free of the pre-
sumed constraints and artificiality of the conventional grid,
Olmsted wrote of his intentions at Riverside: "as the ordinary directness of line in town streets, with its resultant
regularity of plan would suggest eagerness to press forward

... we would recommend ... gracefully curved lines, generous spaces, and the absence of sharp corners, the idea being to suggest and imply leisure, contemplativeness and happy tranquility."

Even so, it is worth recalling that Olmsted designed Riverside not as a resort community remote from the city but more precisely as an independent town that took the city for granted and relied on its rail facilities. Moreover, he imposed controls of his own on the village, including standard lot sizes of 100 by 225 feet and the requirement that houses be set back 30 feet from the street. Many splendid old residences enliven the sweeping, tree-lined drives produced by the plan. Similarly, the center of town is still distinguished by several historic buildings, notably the Chicago, Burlington & Quincy railroad station, its adjacent 108-foot water tower, and an office building executed in the Victorian Gothic manner.

Coonley House (1908)   NR
300 Scottswood, Riverside
Architect: Frank Lloyd Wright

By common agreement, the Avery Coonley House belongs
among the very best of Frank Lloyd Wright's Prairie style
works.

Itself a large building, the house is but a part of an
extensive complex that included a gardener's cottage, a garage, formal gardens, a pool, a service court, and excellent
landscaping throughout.

The house is designed with most of the principal
rooms on a second floor over a raised ground floor.
The massing is extremely complex but forms a unified
whole with nearly every portion liberally sprinkled with

"Wrightian" ornament. The color scheme is dominated by earthen hues, but bits of brilliant red, green, and gold are used for emphasis throughout.

The grounds of the estate no longer exist in their original extent, having been largely disposed of to allow for the construction of new houses. Thus, the house now suffers from crowding by its neighbors.

165

Coonley Playhouse (1912)
350 Fairbank Road, Riverside
Architect: Frank Lloyd Wright

Erected for the family that had commissioned the Coonley House in 1908, the Coonley Playhouse shows Wright in the full confidence of his powers. This small building is monumental in form and intimate in scale. It combines the implied order of a symmetric, cruciform plan with a relaxed and seemingly accidental circulation. The interpenetration of mass and plane are expressed in both the solidity of the enclosing stucco walls and the transparent parade of elements in the art glass windows.

Farnsworth House (1945–50)
Plano
Architect: Ludwig Mies van der Rohe

The Farnsworth House is one of Mies van der Rohe's few completed residential designs in the United States, and by far the most celebrated. It is also Mies's first fully realized example of a unitary space enclosed in a rectangular prism, a building form that more than any other distinguishes his American work from his European.

Architecturally, the house is a remarkable distillate of structure and space: a floor slab and a roof slab are welded to eight wide-flange columns, four to a side, that have been sandblasted to a smooth surface and painted white. The exterior walls are panes of floor-to-ceiling glass hung behind —that is to say, within—the enclosing columns. The slabs are cantilevered from the column rows so that on the western, short side they form an entry porch accessible by a low stair from an asymmetrically oriented terrace, itself reached by another low stair from ground level. While Mies is often

criticized for having paid little attention to the contexts of his buildings, it is worth noting the southern exposure of the house, where the terrace and the house proper effectively embrace a splendid old sugar maple tree that mediates between the manmade and the natural elements.

The main floor slab is poised about 5 feet above the ground to protect the house from occasional flooding from the Fox River, a stream that flows along the front, or southern, edge of the property. This functional attribute, together with the white structure and glass walls, gives the structure a floating, near-apparitional effect.

The interior, which features a core lined mostly in primavera wood, contains kitchen facilities, cabinets, two baths and a fireplace. There is also a freestanding teak closet nearby. So disposed, these elements suggest, without defining, a living-dining area, a sleeping area, and a kitchen area, all linked by unpartitioned space. Mies's practical rationale for so reductivist a design was that the house was commissioned as a country retreat for a single woman, Dr. Edith Farnsworth of Chicago.

The house is isolated on a wooded 9.6 acre tract near Plano, about 50 miles west of Chicago. It is not accessible to the public. During the winter months when the leaves are off the trees, it can be partially glimpsed, at a distance of several hundred yards, from the Silver Springs State Park, on the other side of the Fox River.

167

Ford House   (1950)
404 South Edgelawn, Aurora
Architect: Bruce Goff

The work of Bruce Goff is idiosyncratic, surprising, and pleasing. His house in Aurora, designed in the years after World War II used surplus materials (the metal ribs of the structure came from a quonset hut), unusual materials (marine rope and coal), and fine and rare materials (copper and cyprus). To describe the house as a centralized plan with two symmetric wings is to make it seem unremarkable. To describe it as a pumpkin-shaped building with low walls of coal with large rocklike chunks of glass set in the walls to admit light is to suggest an oddity. While both descriptions are accurate, neither fully conveys the enormously thoughtful and responsive qualities of the building.

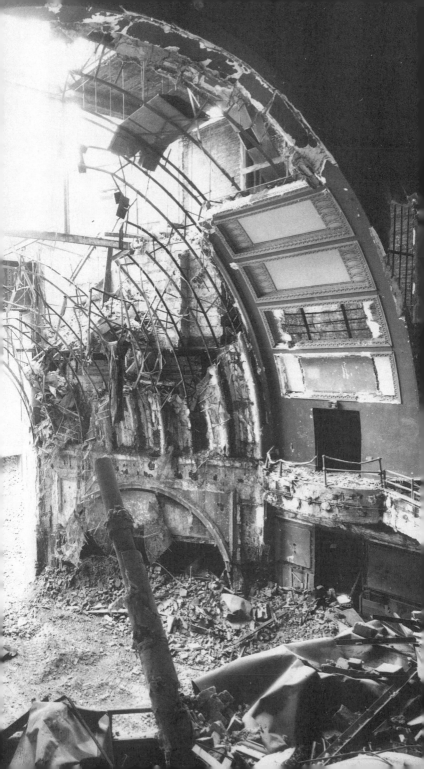

A book such as this has both a celebratory and self-satisfied character. We recognize the great riches the buildings described represent, and we congratulate ourselves on the enduring presence of these buildings, giving as they do so much to the character of this great city. Yet since this book first appeared many of its selections have been destroyed, usually by the enormous forces and pressures of development at work in the center of large cities.

Among the buildings that did not appear in prior editions of this book, some had already been destroyed when the book first appeared, while others had not yet achieved sufficient recognition to have merited their inclusion. This is a highly selective list, in no way encyclopedic or exhaustive. It could be expanded enormously, but we hope that it fairly represents the range of the hurts that citizens have done to themselves. Indifference and neglect are as significant factors in the failures of preservation as care, innovation, and vigilance are in its successes.

We thought that it would have a chastening effect if we reminded ourselves and our readers of the losses we have suffered in order to understand that the great resource represented by buildings cannot be consigned to storage—the way books and paintings that might be out of fashion can be—while awaiting a change of taste or the awakening of appreciation. We believe that buildings are gifts from the past held in trust for the future. We desire that our successors recognize us for our discernment rather than our destructiveness.

The following buildings never appeared in prior editions of this book:

Republic Building (1905–61)
Architects: Holabird & Roche

Federal Building (1905–1966)
Architect: Henry Ives Cobb

Michigan Square Building (1930–73)
Architects: Holabird & Root

Italian Court (1921–69)
Architect: Robert de Golyer

Mecca Flats (1891–1952)
Architect: George Edbrooke

Marshall Field Wholesale Store (1885–1930)
Architect: H. H. Richardson

Walker Warehouse (1888–1953)
Architects: Adler & Sullivan

Midway Gardens (1914–29)
Architect: Frank Lloyd Wright

This group includes buildings listed in earlier editions of this book that have since been destroyed:

Lind Block (1852–1963)
Wacker Drive and Randolph Street
Architect: Unknown

McCarthy Building (1872–1990)
32 West Washington Street
Architect: John Mills Van Osdel

Giles Building (1875–1968)
423–429 South Wabash Avenue
Architect: Otis L. Wheelock

First Leiter Building (1879–1972)
208 West Monroe Street
Architect: William LeBaron Jenney

Hammond Library, Union Theological Seminary
(1882–1963)
Ashland Avenue and Warren Boulevard
Architects: Adler & Sullivan

Hiram Sibley Warehouse (1883–1971)
315–331 North Clark Street
Architect: George H. Edbrooke

First Infantry Armory (1890–1966)
Michigan Avenue and 16th Street
Architects: Burnham & Root

Grand Central Station (1890–1971)
Harrison and Wells streets
Architect: S. S. Beman

Schiller Theater (1892–1961)
64 West Randolph Street
Architects: Adler & Sullivan

Sullivan House (1892–1970)
4575 South Lake Park
Architects: Adler & Sullivan

Meyer Building (1893–1967)
307 West Van Buren Street
Architects: Adler & Sullivan

Yondorf Building (1892–1968)
225–229 South Wacker Drive
Architect: Unknown

Chicago Stock Exchange (1894–1972)
30 North LaSalle Street
Architects: Adler & Sullivan

Francis Apartments (1895–1967)
4304 South Forestville Avenue
Architect: Frank Lloyd Wright

Francisco Terrace (1895–1974)
253–257 North Francisco Avenue
Architect: Frank Lloyd Wright

Cable Building (1899–1961)
57 East Jackson Street
Architects: Holabird & Roche

The Coliseum (1900–1982)
1513 South Wabash Avenue
Architects: Frost & Granger
Engineers: E. C. & R. M. Shankland

Hunter Building (1908–1978)
(later Liberty Mutual Insurance Building)
337 West Madison Street
Architect: Christian A. Eckstorm

Chicago & North Western Station (1911–1984)
West Madison Street
Architects: Frost & Granger

Edison Shop (1912–67)
229 South Wabash Avenue
Architects: Purcell, Feick & Elmslie

Chicago Stadium   (1929–1995)
1800 West Madison Street
Architects: Hall, Lawrence & Ratcliffe

United States Gypsum Building   (1963–1994)
101 South Wacker Drive
Architects: Perkins & Will Partnership

Recently, a building proposed for landmark designation was turned down, in part, because it was not included in this book. While buildings included here are among the most significant in Chicago, it is misleading to conclude that a building is without significance because of its absence from this book.

Abernathy, Ann, and John G. Thorpe. *The Oak Park Home and Studio of Frank Lloyd Wright.* Oak Park: Frank Lloyd Wright Home and Studio Foundation, 1988.

Andreas, A. T. *History of Chicago: From the Earliest Period to the Present Time.* 3 vols. Chicago, 1884–86.

Art Institute of Chicago. *The Plan of Chicago, 1909–1979.* Chicago: Art Institute of Chicago, 1979.

Art Institute of Chicago. *Architecture in context: 360 North Michigan Avenue, the London Guaranty and Accident Company Building, the Stone Container Building.* Chicago: Art Institute of Chicago, 1981.

Art Institute of Chicago. *Chicago Architects Design: A Century of Architectural Drawings from the Art Institute of Chicago.* Chicago: Art Institute of Chicago, 1982.

Art Institute of Chicago. "The Architecture of the Art Institute of Chicago." *Museum Studies* 14, no. 1 (1988).

Bach, Ira J., and Mary Lackritz Gray. *A Guide to Chicago's Public Sculpture.* Chicago: University of Chicago Press, 1983.

Berger, Philip, ed. *Highland Park: American Suburb at Its Best: An Architectural and Historical Survey.* Highland Park: Highland Park Landmark Preservation Committee, 1982.

Block, Jean F. *Hyde Park Houses: An Informal History, 1856–1910.* Chicago: University of Chicago Press, 1978.

———. *The Uses of Gothic: Planning and Building the Campus of the University of Chicago, 1882–1932.* Chicago: University of Chicago Library, 1983.

Bluestone, Daniel M. *Constructing Chicago.* New Haven: Yale University Press, 1991.

Brooks, H. Allen. *The Prairie School: Frank Lloyd Wright and His Midwest Contemporaries.* Toronto: University of Toronto Press, 1973.

Bruegmann, Robert. *Holabird & Roche and Holabird & Root: An Illustrated Catalog of Works, 1880–1940.* New York: Garland, 1991.

Buder, Stanley. *Pullman: An Experiment in Industrial Order and Community Planning, 1880–1930.* New York: Oxford University Press, 1967.

Casari, Maurizio, and Vincenzo Pavan, eds. *New Chicago Architecture: Beyond the International Style.* New York: Rizzoli, 1981.

Chappell, Sally. *Architecture and Planning of Graham, Anderson, Probst and White, 1912–1936.* Chicago: University of Chicago Press, 1992.

Chicago Architectural Club. *Chicago Architectural Journal.*

Chicago Chapter, American Institute of Architects. *Architecture Chicago.*

Chicago Chapter, American Institute of Architects. *AIA Guide to Chicago Architecture.* New York: Harper & Row, 1993.

Cohen, Stuart E. *Chicago Architects: Documenting the Exhibition of the Same Name Organized by Laurence Booth, Stuart E. Cohen, Stanley Tigerman, and Benjamin Weese.* Chicago: Swallow Press, 1976.

Condit, Carl W. *Chicago, 1910–29: Building, Planning, and Urban Technology.* Chicago: University of Chicago Press, 1973.

———. *Chicago, 1930–70: Building, Planning, and Urban Technology.* Chicago: University of Chicago Press, 1974.

———. *The Chicago School of Architecture: A History of Commercial and Public Building in the Chicago Area, 1875–1925.* Chicago: University of Chicago Press, 1964.

Cronon, William. *Nature's Metropolis: Chicago and the Great West.* New York: W. W. Norton, 1991.

Cummings, Kathleen Roy. *Architectural Records in Chicago: A Guide to Architectural Resources in Cook County and Vicinity.* Chicago: Art Institute of Chicago, 1981.

Darling, Sharon. *Chicago Furniture: Art, Craft, and Industry, 1833–1983.* New York: W. W. Norton & Company, 1984.

De Wit, Wim, ed. *Louis Sullivan: The Function of Ornament.* New York: W. W. Norton & Company, 1986.

Drury, John. *Old Chicago Houses.* 1945. Reprint. Chicago: University of Chicago Press, 1975.

Duis, Perry. *Chicago: Creating New Traditions.* Chicago: Chicago Historical Society, 1976.

Eaton, Leonard K. *Two Chicago Architects and Their Clients: Frank Lloyd Wright and Howard Van Doren Shaw.* Cambridge, Mass.: M.I.T. Press, 1969.

Einhorn, Robin L. *Property Rules: Political Economy in Chicago, 1833–1872.* Chicago: University of Chicago Press, 1991.

Fields, Jeanette S., ed. *A Guidebook to the Architecture of River Forest.* River Forest: Architectural Guidebook Committee, River Forest Community Center, 1981.

Frueh, Erne R., and Frueh, Florence. *The Second Presbyterian Church of Chicago: Art and Architecture.* Chicago: Second Presbyterian Church, 1978.

Gapp, Paul. *Paul Gapp's Chicago.* Chicago: Chicago Tribune, 1980.

Grube, Oswald W., Pran, Peter C., and Schulze, Franz. *100 Years of Architecture in Chicago: Continuity of Structure and Form.* Chicago: J. Philip O'Hara, 1976.

Hines, Thomas S. *Burnham of Chicago: Architect and Planner.* New York: Oxford University Press, 1974.

Hirsch, Arnold. *Making the Second Ghetto: Race and Housing in Chicago, 1940–1960.* Cambridge: Cambridge University Press, 1983.

Hoffman, Donald. *The Architecture of John Wellborn Root.* Baltimore: Johns Hopkins University Press, 1973.

————. *Frank Lloyd Wright's Robie House: The Illustrated Story of an Architectural Masterpiece.* New York: Dover, 1984.

Keating, Ann Durkin. *Building Chicago: Suburban Developers and the Creation of a Divided Metropolis.* Columbus: Ohio State University Press, 1988.

Lake Forest Foundation for Historic Preservation. *A Preservation Guide to National Register Properties, Lake Forest, Illinois.* Lake Forest, 1991.

Lane, George. *Chicago Churches and Synagogues: An Architectural Pilgrimage.* Chicago: Loyola University Press, 1981.

Lowe, David. *Lost Chicago.* Boston: Houghton Mifflin Company, 1978.

Manny, Jr., Carter H. *Madlener House: Tradition and Innovation in Architecture.* Chicago: Graham Foundation, 1988.

Manson, Grant Carpenter. *Frank Lloyd Wright to 1910: The First Golden Age.* New York: Van Nostrand Reinhold Company, 1958.

Mayer, Harold M., and Richard C. Wade. *Chicago: Growth of a Metropolis.* Chicago: University of Chicago Press, 1969.

Miller, Ross. *American Apocalypse: The Great Fire and the Myth of Chicago.* Chicago: University of Chicago Press, 1990.

Menocal, Narciso. *Keck and Keck: Architects.* Madison: Elvehjem Museum of Art, 1980.

Molloy, Mary Alice. *Chicago Since the Sears Tower: A Guide to New Downtown Buildings.* Chicago: Inland Architect Press, 1990.

O'Gorman, James F. *Three American Architects: Richardson, Sullivan, and Wright, 1865–1915.* Chicago: University of Chicago Press, 1991.

Pfeiffer, Bruce Brooks, ed. *Frank Lloyd Wright: Collected Writings.* 2 vols. New York: Rizzoli, 1992.

Randall, Frank A. *History of the Development of Building Construction in Chicago.* Urbana: University of Illinois Press, 1949.

Riverside. Frederick Law Olmsted Society. *Riverside: A Village in a Park.* Riverside: Frederick Law Olmsted Society, 1970.

Saliga, Pauline, ed. *The Sky's the Limit: A Century of Chicago Skyscrapers.* New York: Rizzoli, 1990.

Sanderson, Arlene, ed. *Wright Sites: A Guide to Frank Lloyd Wright Public Places.* River Forest: Frank Lloyd Wright Building Conservancy, 1991.

Schulze, Franz. *Mies van der Rohe: A Critical Biography.* Chicago: University of Chicago Press, 1985.

Schulze, Franz, and George E. Danforth, eds. *An Illustrated Catalog of the Mies van der Rohe Drawings in the Museum of Modern Art.* Part II, in 14 vols. New York: Garland, 1993.

Siry, Joseph. *Carson Pirie Scott: Louis Sullivan and the Chicago Department Store.* Chicago: University of Chicago Press, 1988.

Slaton, Deborah, ed. *Wild Onions: A Brief Guide to Landmarks and Lesser-Known Structures in Chicago's Loop.* Chicago: Association for Preservation Technology, 1989.

Smith, Carl S. *Chicago and the American Literary Imagination, 1880–1920.* Chicago: University of Chicago Press, 1984.

Sorell, Victor. *Guide to Chicago Murals, Yesterday and Today.* Chicago: Council on Fine Arts, 1979

Sprague, Paul E. *Guide to Frank Lloyd Wright and Prairie School Architecture in Oak Park.* 2d ed. Oak Park: Village of Oak Park, 1978.

Stamper, John W. *Chicago's North Michigan Avenue: Planning and Development, 1900–1930.* Chicago: University of Chicago Press, 1991.

Storrer, William Allin. *Frank Lloyd Wright Companion.* Chicago: University of Chicago Press, 1993.

Sullivan, Louis H. *The Autobiography of an Idea.* New York: Press of the American Institute of Architects, 1924. Reprinted, New York: Dover Publications, 1956.

Suttles, Gerald D. *The Man-Made City: The Land-Use Confidence Game in Chicago.* Chicago: University of Chicago Press, 1990.

Tallmadge, Thomas E. *Architecture in Old Chicago.* 1941. Reprint. Chicago: University of Chicago Press, 1975.

Twombly, Robert. *Frank Lloyd Wright: His Life and His Architecture.* New York: John Wiley & Sons, 1979.

————. *Louis Sullivan: His Life and Work.* Chicago: University of Chicago Press, 1987.

Wille, Lois. *Forever Open, Clear and Free: The Struggle for Chicago's Lakefront.* 2d ed. Chicago: University of Chicago Press, 1991.

Wright, Frank Lloyd. *An Autobiography.* 3d ed., rev. New York: Horizon Press, 1977.

Wright, Gwendolyn. *Moralism and the Model Home: Domestic Architecture and Cultural Conflict in Chicago, 1873–1913.* Chicago: University of Chicago Press, 1980.

Zukowsky, John, ed. *Chicago Architecture, 1872–1922: Birth of a Metropolis.* Munich: Prestel Verlag, 1987.

————. *Chicago Architecture and Design, 1923–1993: Reconfiguration of an American Metropolis.* Chicago and Munich: Art Institute of Chicago and Prestel Verlag, 1993.

Acroterion The pedestal and the decorated form it supports
capping the corners or the peak of the gable of a
building.

Batter An inward sloped wall plane, usually at the base of a
building.

Caisson An air chamber, resembling a well, driven down to
firm foundation material and filled with concrete.

Cantilevered Built with horizontal beams supported at only
one end and made of material strong enough to resist
collapse at the other end.

Capital The element at the top of a column or of any other
vertical support in a building.

Chamfer The beveled or rounded edge where two surfaces
meet in an exterior or interior angle.

Chicago window A window occupying the full width of
the bay and divided into a large fixed sash flanked by
a narrow movable sash at each side.

Colonnette A small column, often used decoratively rather
than functionally for support.

Corbel A bracket, usually in a group, projecting from a
wall, positioned to receive a load from above.

Corbel table A row of corbels supporting or decorating a
masonry superstructure.

Cornice The projecting horizontal member at the top of a
wall; often a decorative development of the eaves of the
roof.

Cor-ten steel A kind of steel in which natural oxidation has
sealed the surface, protecting it from deterioration.

Cruciform Cross shaped, usually referring to a building
plan.

Cupola A terminal structure, rising above a main roof.

Dentils A series of blocklike projections forming a molding, borrowed from the Greek Ionic order.

Facade The face or front of a building.

Festoon A decorative garland, sculptured in relief as a loop between two points.

Flamboyant Gothic The last phase of French Gothic architecture, notable for the use of flamelike decorative forms, often in the tracery covering large openings.

Gable The upper part of a terminal wall, under the ridge of a pitched roof.

Georgian The architectural style developed during the reigns of Queen Anne and the four Georges, 1702–1830.

Gothic The architecture of the thirteenth, fourteenth, and fifteenth centuries, characterized by the use of pointed arches, buttresses, rib vaulting, and stone tracery.

Guastavino vault A vault characterized by carefully laid tiles; derived from the Catalan masonry tradition.

Helical In the form of a helix, a curve traced on a cylinder by a straight line in a plane wrapped around the cylinder, as in an ordinary screw thread.

Mannerist Referring to the elaborate, highly stylized manner affected by the artists and architects of sixteenth-century Italy

Mansard A roof having a double slope, usually on all four sides, with the lower normally the steeper.

Masonry Construction using plaster, concrete, and the application of stone, brick, tile, etc., sometimes with mortar.

Molding An element of construction or decoration that introduces a variety of outlines or profiles on the edge or surface of a wall.

Mullion An upright division member between a series of windows or doors.

Nave The main portion of a church or cathedral occupied by the worshipers (excluding the transepts).

Ornament Detail applied to plain surfaces of a building, whether by sculpture, incising, painting, or any other method, for the purpose of embellishment.

Palladian window A three-part opening with a flat beam over each side and an arch over the center.

Parapet A low retaining wall at the edge of a roof, porch, or terrace.

Pier Any upright structure used as a principal support by itself or as part of a wall.

Pilaster An engaged pier of shallow depth.

Pile A column driven into the ground as part of a foundation.

Portico An entrance porch.

Romanesque (or Norman) The architecture of Europe ranging in various regional types from about 800 through the twelfth century. It is marked by heavy walls and the use of round arches.

Rosette A circular floral motif, usually carved in stone.

Shear-wall core The element of a tall building designed to take the load of the wind.

Spandrel Originally the three-sided web of material on either side of an arch; over time and by extension, it has been applied to the horizontal panels in the curtain walls of concrete or metal-framed buildings.

Spire A tall tower roof, tapering up to a point.

Stringcourse A continuous horizontal band, plain or molded, on an exterior wall.

Stucco Plaster for exterior walls.

Terra-cotta Cast and fired clay bricks, usually larger and more intricately modeled than bricks.

Trabeation Post-and-lintel or column-and-beam architecture.

Transept Either of the side spaces, perpendicular to the nave and usually separated from it by columns, in a church of cruciform plan.

Trump A form, usually curved, projecting from the wall plane of a building well above the ground, used for stairs or for a stacked series of projecting bays.

Truss A structure made up of a network of members, often in triangular arrangements so as to provide a rigid framework.

Usonian Term invented by Samuel Butler as an alternative to "American," in the sense of "pertaining to the United States," and applied by Frank Lloyd Wright to small, low-cost houses that he designed during the Depression.

Vaulted Roofed by arched masonry, or having the appearance of a roof of arched masonry.

Window hoods A molding or decorative course immediately above a window which projects outward slightly from the main wall plane.

Credits

Some of the photographs in this book illustrate buildings in stages earlier than that of the present. This was done intentionally, to provide the reader with images more instructive of designers' original motives.

Index

335